# Dinosaurs

# A to Z

Jim Pipe

Aladdin/Watts
London • Sydney

© Aladdin Books Ltd 2003

*Produced by:*
Aladdin Books Ltd
28 Percy Street
London W1T 2BZ

ISBN 0-7496-4968-2

*First published in
Great Britain in 2003 by:*
Franklin Watts
96 Leonard Street
London EC2A 4XD

*Editor:*
Katie Harker

*Designer:*
Flick, Book Design & Graphics

*Illustrators:*
James Field, John Butler, Ross Watton, Sarah Smith, Steven Sweet – Simon Girling and Associates. Mike Saunders, Rob Shone, Richard Orr, Peter Barrett, Giovanni Caselli, Richard Rockwood, Mike Lacey, Alan Baker. Wayne Ford, Darren Harvey – Wildlife Art Ltd. Certain illustrations in this book have appeared in previous Aladdin Books titles.

Printed in UAE
All rights reserved

A CIP catalogue record
for this book is available
from the British Library.

The consultant, *Professor Michael Benton,* is head of the Department of Earth Sciences at the University of Bristol, and has written and consulted on books for all ages about dinosaurs and other prehistoric animals.

Aladdin Books would like to thank Flick for this inspired idea.

# ABOUT THIS BOOK

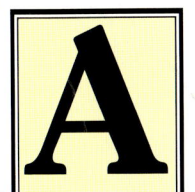

Do you want to know more about a particular dinosaur or another prehistoric animal? Just go to the letter of the dinosaur's name and find your entry alphabetically, or look up your dinosaur in the index to find its page number. You can also use the feature boxes to find dinosaurs that are similar to the one you are looking for. These boxes are listed in the dinosaur family tree on page 94.

Each entry gives the length and weight of the dinosaur (where fossils tell us enough to know), along with a guide to pronunciation and the period in which the dinosaur lived.

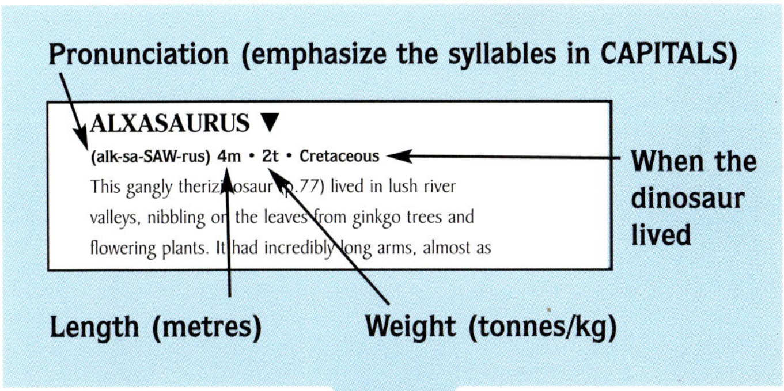

**Pronunciation (emphasize the syllables in CAPITALS)**

**ALXASAURUS ▼**
(alk-sa-SAW-rus) 4m • 2t • Cretaceous
This gangly therizinosaur (p.77) lived in lush river valleys, nibbling on the leaves from ginkgo trees and flowering plants. It had incredibly long arms, almost as

**When the dinosaur lived**

**Length (metres)**   **Weight (tonnes/kg)**

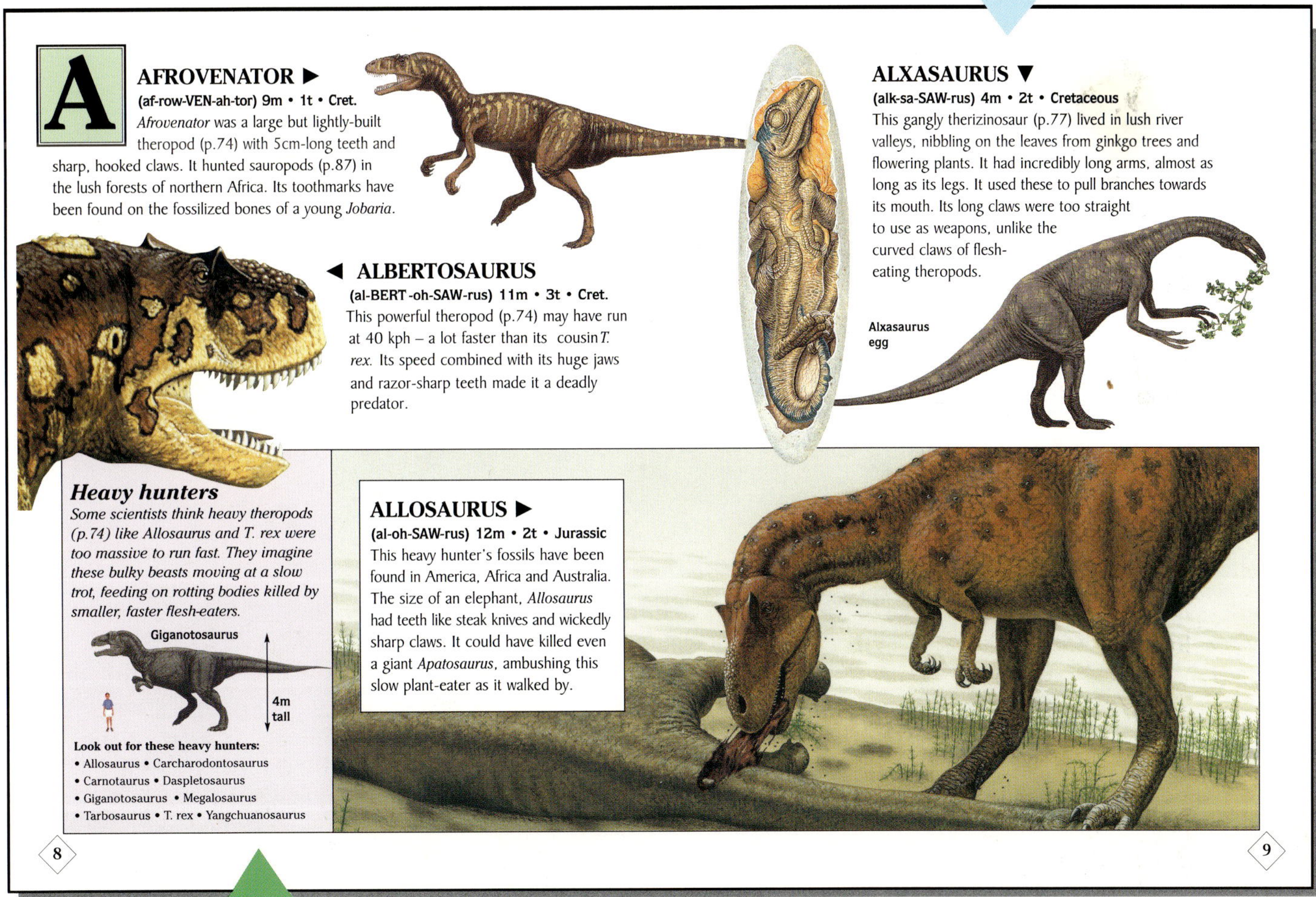

---

### AFROVENATOR ▶
(af-row-VEN-ah-tor) 9m • 1t • Cret.
*Afrovenator* was a large but lightly-built theropod (p.74) with 5cm-long teeth and sharp, hooked claws. It hunted sauropods (p.87) in the lush forests of northern Africa. Its toothmarks have been found on the fossilized bones of a young *Jobaria*.

### ◀ ALBERTOSAURUS
(al-BERT-oh-SAW-rus) 11m • 3t • Cret.
This powerful theropod (p.74) may have run at 40 kph – a lot faster than its cousin *T. rex*. Its speed combined with its huge jaws and razor-sharp teeth made it a deadly predator.

### ALXASAURUS ▼
(alk-sa-SAW-rus) 4m • 2t • Cretaceous
This gangly therizinosaur (p.77) lived in lush river valleys, nibbling on the leaves from ginkgo trees and flowering plants. It had incredibly long arms, almost as long as its legs. It used these to pull branches towards its mouth. Its long claws were too straight to use as weapons, unlike the curved claws of flesh-eating theropods.

*Alxasaurus* egg

### Heavy hunters
Some scientists think heavy theropods (p.74) like *Allosaurus* and *T. rex* were too massive to run fast. They imagine these bulky beasts moving at a slow trot, feeding on rotting bodies killed by smaller, faster flesh-eaters.

Giganotosaurus
4m tall

**Look out for these heavy hunters:**
- Allosaurus • Carcharodontosaurus
- Carnotaurus • Daspletosaurus
- Giganotosaurus • Megalosaurus
- Tarbosaurus • T. rex • Yangchuanosaurus

### ALLOSAURUS ▶
(al-oh-SAW-rus) 12m • 2t • Jurassic
This heavy hunter's fossils have been found in America, Africa and Australia. The size of an elephant, *Allosaurus* had teeth like steak knives and wickedly sharp claws. It could have killed even a giant *Apatosaurus*, ambushing this slow plant-eater as it walked by.

---

### Feature boxes
These boxes focus on different kinds of dinosaur: they include a list of dinosaurs in the same group and a diagram of how big a typical member of the group would be next to a 10-year-old child. Some boxes highlight special characteristics, such as dinosaur brains or dinosaurs with feathers.

# WHAT ARE DINOSAURS?

Dinosaurs were among the most successful animals of all time. These extinct reptiles lived on Earth for about 165 million years – incredible when you think that humans have only been around for about three million years!

The word dinosaur means 'terrible lizard' and like today's reptiles, most had tough, scaly skin and laid eggs. Unlike living reptiles, however, they had straight legs tucked underneath their bodies that enabled them to walk further and move faster than other animals at the time.

**Straight legs**
Today's reptiles, such as crocodiles, have legs that stick out at the sides. But most dinosaurs stood with their legs below their bodies.

◀ Brachiosaurus
Iguanodon ▼
T. rex ▼
Diplodocus ▼
Mamenchisaurus ▲
Human ▲
Styracosaurus ▲

**All shapes and sizes**
This book will help you tell one dinosaur from another. Some dinosaurs were the size of a crow, others weighed over 100 tonnes. Some dinosaurs walked on two legs, others on four; some had claws and fangs, and others had hooves and beaks.

## WHAT DINOSAURS ARE IN THIS BOOK?

Think of all the mammals living today, from whales to pigs and mice. There would have been just as much variety among the dinosaurs. You will find over 120 dinosaurs in this book, as well as many other creatures that lived at the same time, such as birds, fish and flying reptiles. However, no human has seen any of these animals. For this reason, the illustrations in this book are based on careful, scientifically-based guesswork. Further research and new finds may prove that some dinosaurs actually looked very different.

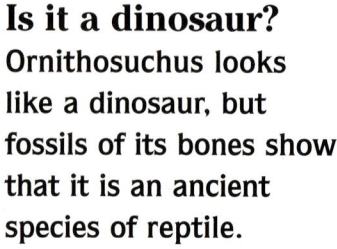

**Is it a dinosaur?**
Ornithosuchus looks like a dinosaur, but fossils of its bones show that it is an ancient species of reptile.

4

▲ Triassic period (250-205 mya)

▲ Jurassic period (205-144 mya)

▲ Cretaceous period (144-65 mya)

▲ Extinction of dinosaurs (65 mya)

## WHEN DID DINOSAURS LIVE?

Dinosaurs lived between 230 and 65 million years ago (mya) in a time known as the Mesozoic era. This is split into three periods: Triassic (p.78), Jurassic (p.42) and Cretaceous (p.22). When the dinosaurs first appeared in the Triassic period, the continents were joined together in one great landmass called Pangaea. Over millions of years, Pangaea split as the continents moved apart very slowly. By the Cretaceous, there were two main continents. In fact, the land continued to move and today we have five continents.

Pangaea ▶ (200 mya)

At the end of each period a mass extinction killed off some species while others replaced them. The world's climate changed over millions of years, too. As a result of these changes, many new plants and animals emerged in each of the three periods. In the Triassic, most dinosaurs were small. By the Jurassic, giant sauropods and plated dinosaurs were dominant, and in the Cretaceous, duckbills, horned dinosaurs and massive hunters like *T. rex* appeared.

## WHERE DID THEY GO?

The Cretaceous period ended with a bang. It now seems clear that a huge meteorite hit the Earth 65 mya, causing global fires and large clouds of dust that blotted out the sun and made the Earth very cold and dark. This would have killed off many plant species – the main food source for dinosaurs. Only small creatures like mammals and birds would have been able to survive in such harsh conditions. Consequently, the dinosaurs disappeared, along with all flying reptiles and most marine reptiles.

5

# HOW DO WE KNOW ABOUT DINOSAURS?

Fossils give us clues to the life of dinosaurs. They are the remains of plants and animals that have been preserved in rock. Dinosaur scientists, called palaeontologists, dig up dinosaur bones. But it is a long and difficult business – even giant dinosaur bones are very fragile. Once a skeleton has been found, it has to be removed from the hard rock, then cleaned and preserved so it doesn't fall apart.

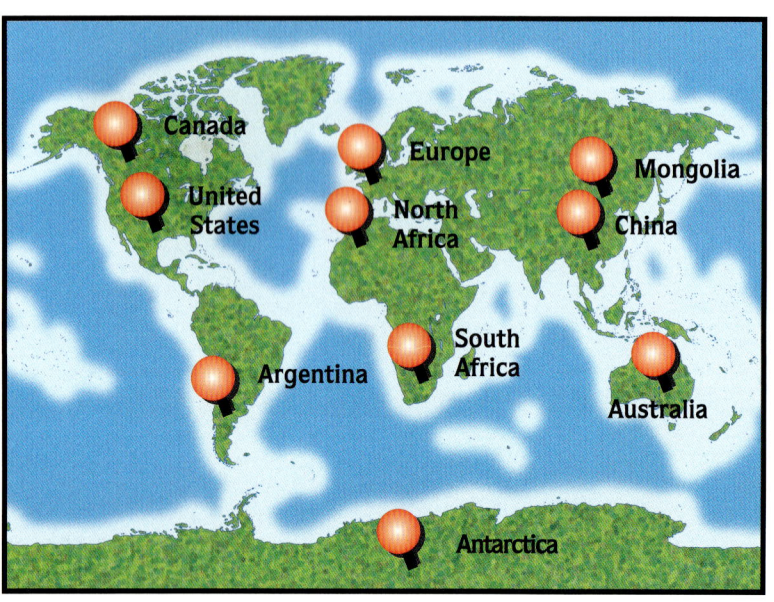

◀ **Where have dinosaur fossils been found?**
Dinosaur fossils have been found all over the world: the map on the left shows the major sites. In recent years, sites in China have produced many exciting finds, due to the unusual rock formations which have preserved fur, feathers and the bones of small animals.

**How did a dinosaur become a fossil?** ▶
1  A dead dinosaur's flesh would normally have been eaten by meat-eating animals and the bones rotted.
2  However, the bones of dinosaurs that got buried under layers of sand or mud turned into fossils, as tiny spaces in the bones filled with rock.
3  Millions of years later, the fossilized bones are uncovered by water or wind action.

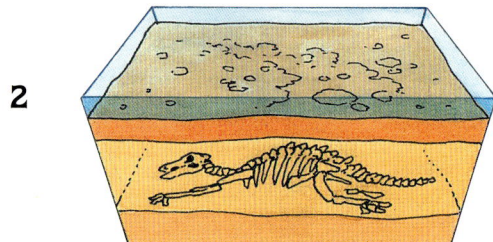

**How do we know when a dinosaur lived?**
Scientists can work out when a dinosaur lived by studying the rock formations in which fossils are found, or by finding common fossils nearby. The natural radioactivity in rocks can also give clues to their age.

6

# WHAT COULD WE STILL FIND OUT?

We know very little about how the insides of a dinosaur really worked, because fossils only preserve the hard parts of an animal. However, scientists are constantly making exciting discoveries that are changing our view of dinosaurs. Only very recently, small, flesh-eating dinosaurs were found covered in feathers, like birds, and some scientists think that even large dinosaurs may have had downy fur while they were young.

### Dinosaur skin ▶

For a long time, scientists have known that dinosaurs had scaly skin, while some even had big bone plates set in the skin, just like modern crocodiles. Fossils have shown these plates and scales pressed into the rock.

However, we have only been able to guess the colour of dinosaurs. Scientists think that, like tigers today, many dinosaurs were probably coloured so they could blend in with their surroundings. Others may have had bright feathers like a parrot!

### ◀ How many dinosaurs are there?

About 1,000 dinosaurs have been found so far, but there could have been over 10,000 types, or species, of dinosaurs. Small animals are less likely to survive as fossils, so there are probably many smaller dinosaurs the size of Microraptor (left) yet to be discovered.

### Matching bones ▶

We are improving our ability to identify prehistoric animals all the time. It is now becoming much easier to identify similar bones that are found in many different parts of the world. For example, scientists believe that Suchomimus, discovered in 1997, may be just a large Baryonyx (right).

7

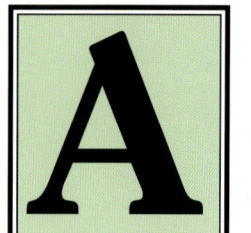

### AFROVENATOR ▶
(af-row-VEN-ah-tor) 9m • 1t • Cret.
*Afrovenator* was a large but lightly-built theropod (p.74) with 5cm-long teeth and sharp, hooked claws. It hunted sauropods (p.87) in the lush forests of northern Africa. Its toothmarks have been found on the fossilized bones of a young *Jobaria*.

### ◀ ALBERTOSAURUS
(al-BERT-oh-SAW-rus) 11m • 3t • Cret.
This powerful theropod (p.74) may have run at 40 kph – a lot faster than its cousin *T. rex*. Its speed combined with its huge jaws and razor-sharp teeth made it a deadly predator.

### *Heavy hunters*
*Some scientists think heavy theropods (p.74) like Allosaurus and T. rex were too massive to run fast. They imagine these bulky beasts moving at a slow trot, feeding on rotting bodies killed by smaller, faster flesh-eaters.*

Giganotosaurus

4m tall

**Look out for these heavy hunters:**
- Allosaurus • Carcharodontosaurus
- Carnotaurus • Daspletosaurus
- Giganotosaurus • Megalosaurus
- Tarbosaurus • T. rex • Yangchuanosaurus

### ALLOSAURUS ▶
(al-oh-SAW-rus) 12m • 2t • Jurassic
This heavy hunter's fossils have been found in America, Africa and Australia. The size of an elephant, *Allosaurus* had teeth like steak knives and wickedly sharp claws. It could have killed even a giant *Apatosaurus*, ambushing this slow plant-eater as it walked by.

# ALXASAURUS ▼

**(alk-sa-SAW-rus) 4m • 2t • Cretaceous**

This gangly therizinosaur (p.77) lived in lush river valleys, nibbling on the leaves from ginkgo trees and flowering plants. It had incredibly long arms, almost as long as its legs. It used these to pull branches towards its mouth. Its long claws were too straight to use as weapons, unlike the curved claws of flesh-eating theropods.

**Alxasaurus egg**

## ◀ AMARGASAURUS

(a-MAR-ga-SAW-rus) 10m • 2t • Cretaceous

This unusual sauropod (p.87) had pairs of spines that ran down its back. These held up an amazing sail that protected *Amargasaurus'* neck. Males may have also used this 'sail' to show off to females, pumping blood into it until it went bright red.

## Armoured dinosaurs

This group of four-legged plant-eating dinosaurs, called 'ankylosaurs', were 3-10m long and up to 2m wide. They were too slow to run from danger and had only stubby claws, but they were built like tanks! Their back, neck and tail were protected by massive bony plates and spikes set in a thick, leathery skin.

6m long
Talarurus

**Look out for these armoured dinosaurs:**
- *All plated dinosaurs (p.44)* • Ankylosaurus
- Dyoplosaurus • Edmontonia • Euoplocephalus
- Hylaeosaurus • Minmi • Nodosaurus • Polacanthus
- Sauropelta • Scelidosaurus • Talarurus

Ankylosaur

## ANKYLOSAURUS ▶

(an-KIE-loh-SAW-rus) 10m • 4t • Cret.

*Ankylosaurus* was as big as a tank and just as heavily armoured – even its eyelids were plated with bone (right). Like other ankylosaurs, it needed to eat huge amounts of ground-hugging plants each day to keep itself alive.

# ANTARCTOSAURUS ▼
**(ant-ARK-toh-SAW-rus) 18m • 40t • Cret.**
This sauropod (p.87) was armoured like *Saltasaurus*. It had big eyes in a small head, with just a few peg-like teeth at the front of its jaws.

# ANUROGNATHUS ▼
**(ah-NEW-rog-NAY-thus) 0.5m • 2kg • Jur.**
This small, fast-flying pterosaur (p.60) used its sharp, pointed teeth to catch insects in mid-air. Some *Anurognathus* may have lived on the giant sauropods, feeding on insects that sucked their blood.

# APATOSAURUS ▶
**(ah-PAT-oh-SAW-rus) 23m • 30t • Jurassic**
To sustain its immense body, *Apatosaurus* must have eaten almost non-stop, stuffing huge amounts of food into its narrow mouth. This sauropod (p.87) had a mixed diet of ferns and tree leaves, which it reached using its long neck. Scientists used to call this dinosaur *Brontosaurus*, until they realized in 1975 that the *Brontosaurus* and *Apatosaurus* fossils were the same animal. So if you're looking for a *Brontosaurus*, you've found it!

# ARCHAEOPTERYX ▼

**(AR-key-OP-ter-iks) 1m across • 1kg • Jurassic**

*Archaeopteryx* is the oldest known bird. The size of a crow, it had the wings of a bird but the teeth, claws and bony tail of a reptile. It was not a good flyer, but with its long legs it could leap off the ground to grab insects.

# ARCHELON ▲

**(ark-eh-LON) 4m • 2t • Cret.**

Sea turtles first appeared during the Cretaceous period. *Archelon* was one of the biggest — it was the size of a car and twice as big as any living turtle. Like modern turtles, it swam using its large paddles and came onshore to lay its eggs. Its tough shell was its only protection against large marine predators such as *Kronosaurus* or *Elasmosaurus*.

**Avimimus could have folded its arms like a bird folds its wings.**

# AVIMIMUS ▶

**(ay-vee-MEEM-us) 1.5m • 15kg • Cretaceous**

Like a roadrunner today, this theropod (p.74) scampered after small animals on its long legs, bobbing down to seize them in its long, toothless beak. It may have had feathers (p.13), but its short 'wings' would have been too weak for flying.

# B

## BAGACERATOPS ▼
(bag-uh-SER-ah-tops) 1m • 30kg • Cretaceous

This rugged horned dinosaur (p.19) lived in the dry, dusty plains of Mongolia and was about the same size as a sheep. It had no teeth, but had a tough beak to nip off leaves and branches. It laid its eggs in an underground nest dug into the sand dunes.

Bagaceratops' horned head had a slender frill at the back.

## Feathered theropods

Recent discoveries in China proved once and for all that birds are descendants of theropod dinosaurs (p.74)! Fossils of dinosaurs called 'fuzzy' raptors have been found with downy fur and feathers.

Look out for these feathered theropods:
- Avimimus
- Bambiraptor
- Caudipteryx
- Incisivosaurus
- Microraptor
- Sinosauropteryx

## BAMBIRAPTOR ▼
(BAM-bee-rap-tor) 1m • 3kg • Cret.

This fuzzy theropod (p.74) was found by 14-year-old Wes Linster in Montana, USA, in 1994. Its name comes from the Italian word 'bambino', meaning baby. It was actually a flesh-eater that used its speed and agility to hunt frogs and other small animals. *Bambiraptor* was similar to the ancient bird *Archaeopteryx*. It had a wishbone like a bird, and if its long arms had been covered in feathers, it could have flown!

# BAROSAURUS ▶

(bar-oh-SAW-rus) 27m • 23t • Jur.

This sauropod's neck made up a third of its length! By rearing up on its hind legs, it could use its massive bulk to crush an attacker. In this position, its head would have been 15m above ground!

# BAVARISAURUS ▼

(ba-VA-ree-SAW-rus) 50cm • 2kg • Jur.

This small lizard would have been a tasty meal for smaller dinosaur predators. Its whole skeleton was found inside the ribcage of a *Compsognathus* – it was the dinosaur's last meal!

Bavarisaurus skeleton

# BARYONYX ▼

(bar-ee-ON-iks) 9m • 2t • Cretaceous

*Baryonyx* (meaning 'heavy claw') was a weird-looking theropod (p.74) armed with long crocodile-like jaws and giant hooked thumb claws. It used these to catch fish in the swamps of Cretaceous Europe.

# BRACHIOSAURUS ▲

**(BRAK-ee-oh-SAW-rus) 30m • 54t • Jurassic**

Though it was not the longest sauropod (p.87), *Brachiosaurus*' thick bones made it one of the heaviest. It moved its neck like a long crane, stretching up to rip leaves from trees the height of a four-storey building, or bending down to shred low-lying ferns with its chisel-shaped teeth.

When a *Brachiosaurus* herd roamed in search of food, small pterosaurs like *Anurognathus* hitched a ride, feeding on insects that sucked the sauropod's blood. On the ground, hordes of beetles fed on its freshly-laid dung.

# CAMARASAURUS ▶

**(ka-MAR-ah-SAW-rus) 18m • 18t • Jurassic**

This colossal plant-eater lived in North America. Like all sauropods (p.87), it had the pillar-like legs and stubby feet of an elephant. *Camarasaurus* had a much shorter neck than *Diplodocus,* but its bulldog-like muzzle was filled with strong, spoon-shaped teeth that could munch tough twigs as well as soft leaves. *Camarasaurus'* keen eyes and sensitive nose detected lurking predators, and its size and sharp thumb claws protected it against all but the biggest flesh-eaters.

# C

## CARCHARODONTOSAURUS ▼
(kar-kar-oh-DON-toh-SAW-rus)
14m • 7t • Cretaceous

Discovered in 1995 in the Atlas Mountains of Africa, this heavy hunter (p.8) could have killed very large prey indeed. It was perhaps even bigger than *T. rex*, though the shape of its 1.6m-long skull shows that it had a smaller brain. Its name means 'shark-toothed lizard'.

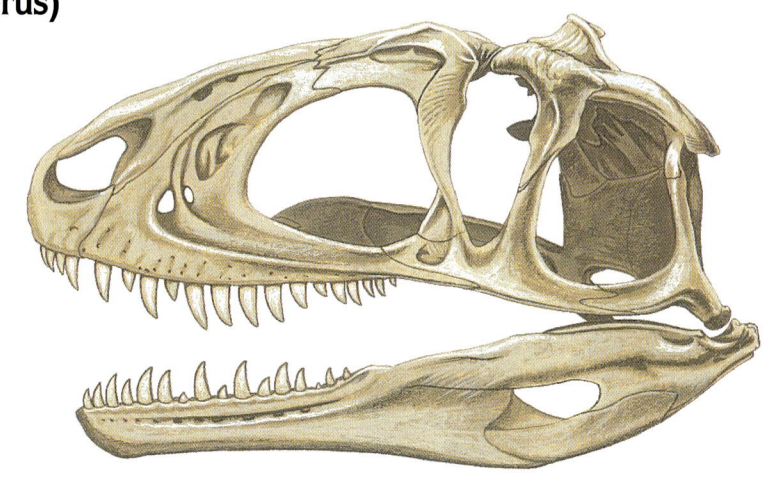
**Carcharodontosaurus skull**

## ◄ CARNOTAURUS
(kar-noh-TAW-rus) 7.5m • 1t • Cretaceous

It's easy to see why this heavy hunter's (p.8) name means 'meat-eating bull' – it had two pointed horns above its eyes. Males may have used these in fights over females. Like *T. rex*, *Carnotaurus* walked on two huge hind legs, had small arms, and probably fed on dead animals as well as live prey. *Carnotaurus* fossils show that thousands of overlapping scales covered its body and larger cone-like scales formed rows along its back.

## CAUDIPTERYX ►
(kaw-DIP-ter-iks) 70cm tall • Cret.

This strange, turkey-sized theropod (p.74) couldn't fly, but it had long feathers sprouting from its arms and tail (p.13). Long legs would have made it a fast runner, and its clawed hands and toothed beak were ideal for hunting insects, frogs and small lizards.

# Horned dinosaurs

This group of four-legged plant-eaters grew up to 9m long. They lived in herds and spent most of the day nibbling at plants like giant sheep! Bony frills and nose horns protected them against predators, and they probably charged at attackers like a bull! Males also used their horns in shoving contests against other males.

**Look out for these horned dinosaurs:**
- Bagaceratops • Centrosaurus
- Einiosaurus • Protoceratops
- Psittacosaurus • Styracosaurus
- Triceratops

**Styracosaurus**

2.7m tall

## CENTROSAURUS ▶
(sen-troh-SAW-rus)

6m • 2.5t • Cretaceous

Like a rhinoceros, this stocky plant-eater had a long, curved horn on its snout, big shoulders and short, powerful legs. It also had a large frill around its neck.

*Centrosaurus* lived in the swamps and rivers of what is now Canada. Like most horned dinosaurs, it had an incredibly strong bite and its long cheek teeth worked like scissors to cut up tough plants.

# CERATOSAURUS ▼
**(seh-RAT-oh-SAW-rus) 6m • 1t • Jurassic**
This swift, powerful theropod (p.74) had a small, bony horn on its head. But its weapons were its giant fangs and bone-crunching jaws. Hunting in packs (p.25) it could have killed an adult *Apatosaurus*. Fossilized tracks on a riverbed also show it was a good swimmer!

A pack of Ceratosaurus attack an Apatosaurus.

# CETIOSAURUS ▼
**(see-tee-oh-SAW-rus) 15m • 22t • Jur.**
When scientists found the first fossils of *Cetiosaurus* in 1841, they thought it was a whale that swam by waggling its tail. Twenty years later they found a more complete skeleton and realised it was a sauropod (p.87)!

# ◄ COELOPHYSIS
**(SEE-low-FIE-sis) 3m • 60kg • Triassic**
*Coelophysis* appeared in the late Triassic period and is one of the earliest-known theropods (p.74). It may have hunted in packs (p.25), scampering about on its long hind legs and jabbing at prey with its flexible, S-shaped neck. Fossils show that it was a cannibal that might have eaten its own young!

# COMPSOGNATHUS ▼
(komp-sog-NAY-thus) 1m • 3.5kg • Jur.
This small theropod (p.74) had a slim, bird-like body with a narrow head and a long tail. Amazingly, it may have been one of the biggest predators on the warm desert islands on which it lived. A fast runner, it hunted lizards like *Bavarisaurus*, and possibly ate crabs and fish that washed ashore. It could have attacked much larger animals by hunting in packs (p.25).

# CONFUCIUSORNIS ▼
(con-FYOO-shu-SOR-nis)
60cm • 1kg • Cretaceous 
This magpie-sized bird lived in China over 120 million years ago. It lived in large flocks and nested in the trees. It ate plants with its toothless beak. Male birds had long tail feathers while females had short stubby tails.

# CORYTHOSAURUS ▶
(ko-RITH-oh-SAW-rus) 10m • 4t • Cretaceous
This well-known duckbill dinosaur (p.82) roamed the plains of North America, browsing on leaves, fruits and flowering plants. It lived in herds that mixed with other duckbill dinosaurs. Its name means 'helmet lizard' and comes from the spectacular crest on its head.

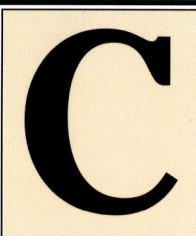

# CRETACEOUS PERIOD

The Cretaceous period lasted from 144 to 65 million years ago, and ended with the extinction of the dinosaurs (p.5). During this time, the oceans split up the big continents and the world grew warmer and drier. Flowering plants appeared along with many new types of dinosaur, including heavy hunters like *Carnotaurus*, armoured dinosaurs like *Styracosaurus* and duckbill plant-eaters such as *Lambeosaurus*. Dinosaurs still ruled the land, but the first snakes, moths and bees appeared as well as many new kinds of small mammal. Aeroplane-sized pterosaurs (p.60) like *Quetzalcoatlus* soared overhead and enormous marine reptiles such as *Tylosaurus* terrorized the shallow oceans.

# CRYOLOPHOSAURUS ▶

**(cry-oh-LOAF-oh-SAW-rus) 6m • 300kg • Jurassic**

This theropod (p.74) lived near the South Pole. The Polar regions were much warmer then than today, but *Cryolophosaurus* had to survive cold winters and endless night for six months a year. It has been nicknamed 'Elvisaurus' because its crest looked like Elvis Presley's hairstyle!

# CYNOGNATHUS ▲

**(sy-nog-NAY-thus) 1m • 40kg • Triassic**

This animal was one of the largest cynodonts. These hairy, mammal-like creatures lived alongside early dinosaurs during the Triassic period. This group of reptiles lasted for about 80 million years until the early Jurassic period.

*Cynognathus* was the size of a large dog, with powerful jaws that could deliver a crushing bite. It was also one of the first animals that could chew its food, enabling it to eat a varied diet. It hunted plant-eating cynodonts, and other lizard-sized amphibians and reptiles.

# D

## DACENTRURUS ▼
(dah-sen-TROO-rus) 4.5m • 4t • Jurassic

This small plated dinosaur (p.44) had a narrow head, short teeth for eating soft plants and two rows of spikes along its back. It lashed out with its spiky tail to defend itself.

## DASPLETOSAURUS ▼
(das-PLEET-oh-SAW-rus) 9m • 4t • Cret.

This heavy hunter's (p.8) name means 'frightful lizard'. It was a relative of *T. rex*, but had larger arms and tiny horns behind its eyes. It hunted plant-eaters like *Stegoceras* in marshy areas near rivers.

## Pack hunters
*Small and medium-sized theropods (p.74) were the ultimate killing machines. These clever dinosaurs (p.81) hunted in packs like wolves. They swarmed over their prey, slashing with their sharp claws until their victim collapsed from loss of blood.*

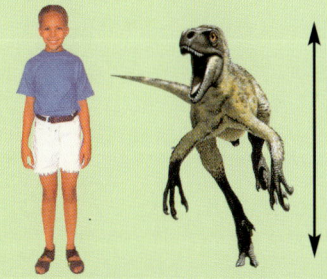

0.8m tall

Velociraptor

**Look out for these pack hunters:**
- Ceratosaurus • Coelophysis
- Compsognathus • Deinocheirus
- Deinonychus • Deltadromeus
- Megaraptor • Noasaurus • Troodon
- Utahraptor • Variraptor • Velociraptor

## DEINOCHEIRUS ▼
(die-noh-KIE-rus) 9m • 6t • Cret.

Imagine a giant hunter as big as *T. rex*, but with arms 2.5 metres long and claws like long kitchen knives. Then make it an incredibly fast runner that hunted in packs – and you would have *Deinocheirus*!

25

# D

## DEINONYCHUS ▼

**(die-NON-ih-kuss) 3m • 80kg • Cretaceous**

*Deinonychus* wasn't the biggest predator in the dinosaur world, but few theropods could match its awesome killing power when it hunted in packs (p.25). This clever hunter (p.81) was armed with sharp, curved fangs and vicious claws sprouted from its fingers and toes.

*Deinonychus*' scaly or feathered skin may have been spotted like a leopard's to help it stalk its prey. Its stiff tail kept it balanced as it leapt into the attack and the huge swivelling claws on its second toe slashed at its victim, easily piercing the tough, scaly hides of most plant-eaters.

## DELTADROMEUS ◀
(del-tah-DROM-ee-us) 8m • 4t • Cret.
This fast-moving theropod was two-thirds as long as *T. rex* and a lot lighter. It may have hunted in packs (p.25) in the swampy forests of North Africa.

## DIMORPHODON ▼
(die-MORF-oh-don) 1.5m across • 12kg • Jur.
This early pterosaur (p.60) had a huge skull and a beak filled with long and short teeth which it used to catch insects, lizards and fish. It may have hunted on all fours.

## DIPLODOCUS ▼
(di-PLOD-oh-kus) 27m • 20t • Jurassic
*Diplodocus* was longer than a tennis court, but due to its hollow bones this sauropod (p.87) weighed no more than four large elephants. Its long neck was too stiff to raise high, so it fed on low-growing ferns. It had a small head and peg-shaped teeth.

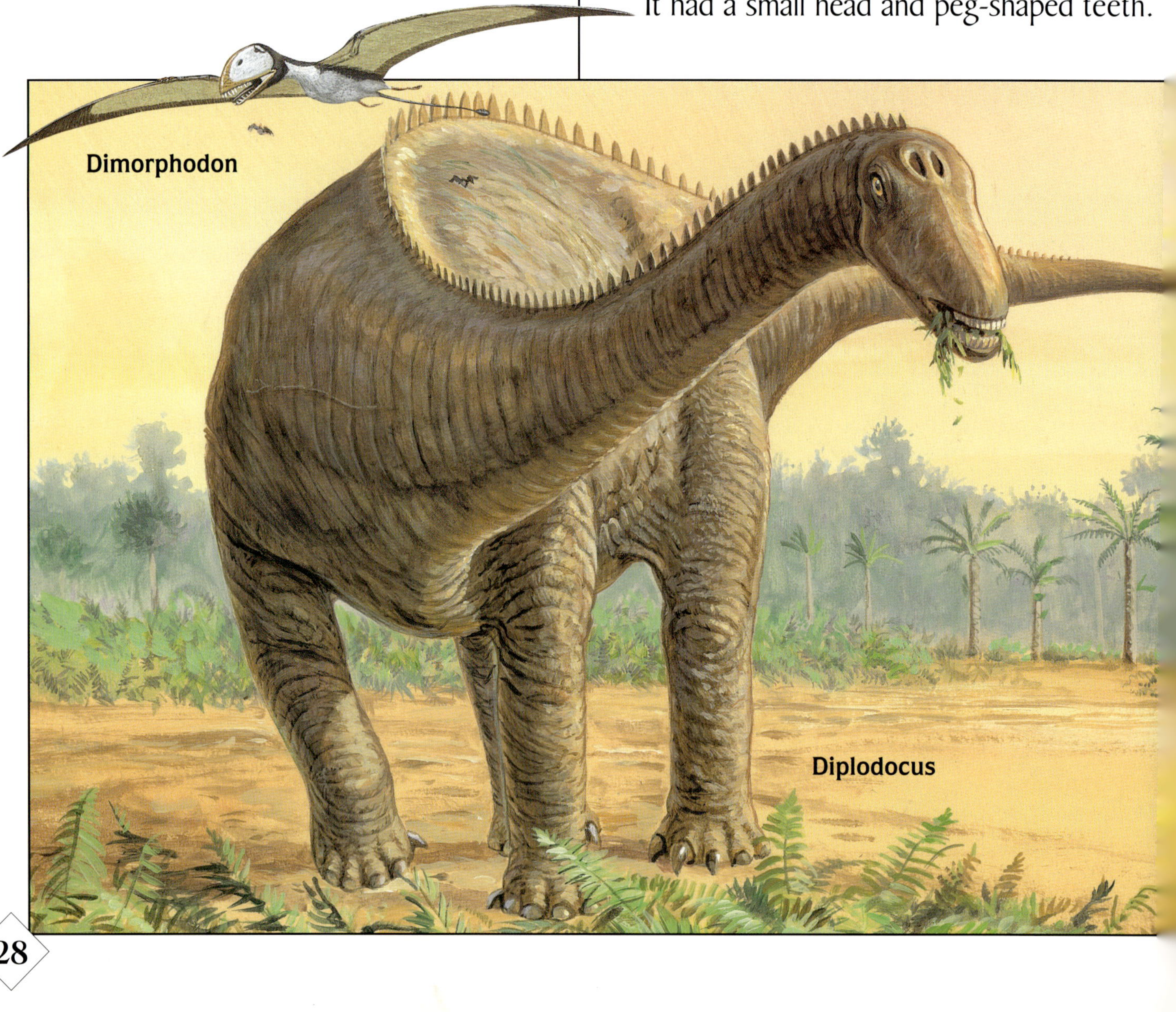

Dimorphodon

Diplodocus

## Ornithopods: feet like a bird!

This family of two-legged plant-eaters had feet like a bird, a horny beak and cheek teeth for slicing and chewing plants. Early Jurassic ornithopods like Lesothosaurus were small, but developed into huge duckbills like Edmontosaurus by the Cretaceous period.

**Look out for these ornithopods:**
- *All duckbills (p.82)*
- Dryosaurus • Fabrosaurus
- Heterodontosaurus
- Hypsilophodon • Iguanodon
- Lesothosaurus • Muttaburrasaurus
- Tenontosaurus • Thescelosaurus
- Xiaosaurus • Yandusaurus • Zephyrosaurus

Zephyrosaurus 1.8m tall

## DRYOSAURUS ▼
(dry-oh-SAW-rus) 4m • 1t • Jur.

This common ornithopod's name means 'oak lizard', because it had teeth shaped like oak leaves. It grazed on leaves and ferns in the forests of North America, Africa and Europe. *Dryosaurus* herds migrated long distances in search of food. Its long legs made it a fast runner able to sprint from danger.

Diplodocus' main defence was its size. It also had an incredibly long tail, which it used to whip attackers.

## DSUNGARIPTERUS ▼
(zung-ga-RIP-ter-us)
3m across • 10 kg • Cretaceous
This pterosaur's (p.60) large, leathery wings enabled it to fly long distances. It hunted for fish, crabs and other sea creatures, using the flat teeth at the back of its jaws to crush shells.

## DYOPLOSAURUS ▼
(die-oh-ploh-SAW-rus)  7m • 10t • Cret.
Like *Euoplocephalus*, *Dyoplosaurus* was a heavily-armoured plant-eating dinosaur (p.10) with a bony club on its tail and a body covered in thick armour plates and spines. It was found in Alberta, Canada.

# E

## ECHIOCERAS ▼
(ek-ee-oh-SER-ass) 6cm • Cret.
*Echioceras* was an ammonite, an ancient relative of the squid that grew inside a flat-sided, coiled shell. *Echioceras* squirted water one way to push itself in the opposite direction. It was a popular meal for sea hunters like *Mosasaurus*.

## EDMONTONIA ▼
(ed-mon-TOH-nee-ah) 6m • 10t • Cret.
Twice the weight of a modern rhino, this armoured plant-eater (p.10) had a tiny head. Its massive body was covered in large bony plates and giant spikes sprouted from its sides. To defend itself or its young, it may have charged at predators such as *Albertosaurus*.

## EDMONTOSAURUS ▼
**(ed-MON-toh-SAW-rus) 13m • 4t • Cret.**
This large duckbill plant-eater (p.82) lived in slow-moving herds in what is now Canada. It may have migrated thousands of kilometres a year, moving north in spring and south again in winter. It usually walked on all fours, but may have reared up on its hind legs to run from danger.

## EINIOSAURUS ▲
**(EYE-nee-oh-SAW-rus) 6m • 3t • Cret.**
This horned dinosaur (p.19) had a short, curved horn on its snout. An adult *Einiosaurus* used this horn to fight off big flesh-eaters. Adults also protected their young by bunching together and forming a wall of horns to shield their offspring.

31

# ELASMOSAURUS ▼

(ee-LAZ-moh-SAW-rus) 14m • 10.5t • Cret.
This undersea hunter belonged to a group of long-necked reptiles called 'plesiosaurs'. It could plunge its 5m-long neck into a shoal of fish or lower it down to the sea floor to grab ammonites or crabs. It used its wing-like flippers to 'fly' through the water, pushing them down and back before bringing them up and forwards in a loop.

# ERLIKOSAURUS ▼

(er-LICK-oh-SAW-rus) 5m • 200kg • Cret.
Erlikosaurus' skull provides important clues to understanding the mysterious therizinosaurs (p.77). The small, pointed teeth show that they were plant-eaters, unusual among theropod dinosaurs.

Erlikosaurus skull

# EORAPTOR ▶

(EE-oh-RAP-tor)
1m • 4kg • Triassic
This theropod (p.74) lived about 228 million years ago in what is now Argentina. It is one of the oldest dinosaurs we know about. The size of a small dog, it probably hunted lizards and small mammal-like animals.

# EUOPLOCEPHALUS ▼

**(YOU-oh-plo-SEF-ah-lus) 6m • 3t • Cretaceous**

This armoured dinosaur (p.10) wandered through the forests of North America in herds, browsing on low-lying plants. Studs, spikes and large horny plates covered its body and its stiff tail ended in a huge, bony club. It was very agile for such a big animal. If attacked, it could spin around and deliver a crushing blow to its enemy.

# F

## Dinosaur hips

All dinosaurs belong to one of two groups, depending on their hips! 'Lizard hips' (saurischia) had three bones pointing in different directions. 'Bird hips' (ornithischia) had both of the lower bones pointing backwards.

'Bird hips'

'Lizard hips'

## ◀ FABROSAURUS

(FAB-roh-SAW-rus) • 1m • 70kg • Jur.

This small ornithopod (p.29) was one of the first dinosaurs with 'bird hips' and walked around on its hind legs. Like deer, it lived in herds and used its speed to sprint from danger.

# G

## GALLIMIMUS ▶

(gall-ee-MEEM-us)
6m • 120kg • Cretaceous

*Gallimimus* was the largest of the speedy 'ostrich' dinosaurs (p.72). As well as long legs, this theropod (p.74) had three-fingered hands for grasping leaves, small mammals and lizards. Big eyes on the sides of its small, bird-like head could spot attackers coming from most directions.

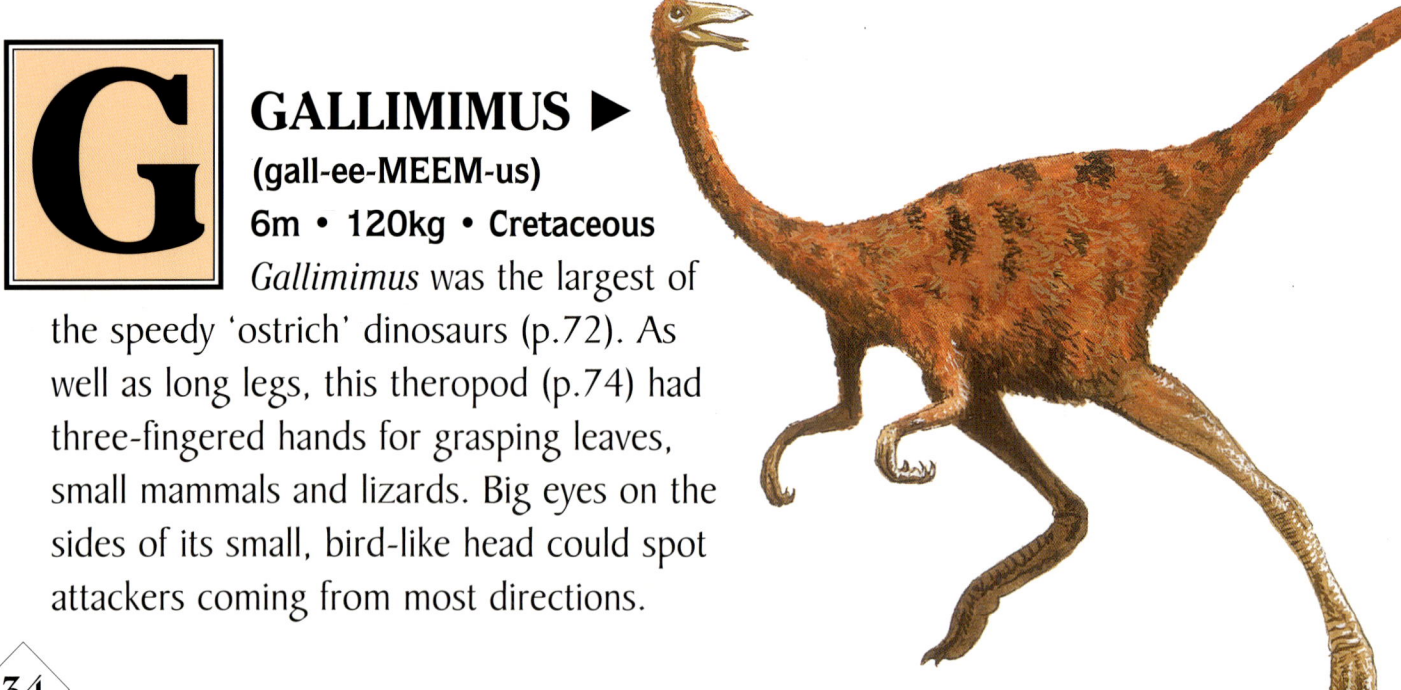

34

## GASOSAURUS ▶
(GAS-oh-SAW-rus)

4m • 300kg • Jurassic

This theropod (p.74) had short arms, powerful legs, a stiff, pointed tail and big jaws with sharp teeth. *Gasosaurus* is named after the gas company workers that found its fossils in a quarry in China.

## GERROTHORAX ▼
(ge-ROH-thor-aks) 1m • Triassic

This funny-looking creature was not a dinosaur, but a flesh-eating amphibian that hunted fish and other small animals in rivers and lakes. It looked like an enormous tadpole with a flattened body, a short, wide head and two small eyes close together. It paddled along using its webbed hind limbs and tail.

## GIGANOTOSAURUS ▲
(ji-GA-noh-toh-SAW-rus)

14m • 7t • Cretaceous

This heavy hunter (p.8) was perhaps an even bigger brute than *T. rex*. It certainly had stronger arms and massively powerful legs. Its head was twice the size of an *Allosaurus*' head, with a bony crest. Its fangs were 20cm long.

# H

## HERRERASAURUS ▼
(eh-ray-rah-SAW-rus)
4m • 200kg • Triassic

One of the earliest known dinosaurs, *Herrerasaurus* was a two-legged theropod (p.74). It was larger than most dinosaurs of its day and a swift runner. Using its sharp claws and pointed teeth it preyed on slow four-legged plant-eaters in the Argentinian plains.

## HESPERORNIS ▼
(HESS-per-OR-niss) 2m long • Cret.

This huge, long-necked seabird couldn't fly but was a strong swimmer. It used its large, webbed feet to push it through the water, and it grabbed fish in its toothy beak.

## HETERODONTOSAURUS ▼
(HET-er-oh-DONT-oh-SAW-rus)
1m • 70kg • Jurassic

The size of a large turkey, this speedy ornithopod (p.29) searched for plants in the dry scrub of South Africa. It may have dug up roots with the sharp claws on its two inside fingers. It had three kinds of teeth, some for chewing plants and others for stabbing enemies.

Heterodontosaurus may have had bright markings on its skin like a modern gazelle.

# HOMALOCEPHALE ▼
(HOME-ah-loh-SEFF-ah-lee) 3m • 150kg • Cret.
This bonehead dinosaur (p.51) had a flat head which males may have used to butt rivals. It also had such wide hips that scientists believe females gave birth to live young, rather than laying eggs like most dinosaurs (p.48).

# HUAYANGOSAURUS ▼
(hoo-ah-YANG-oh-SAW-rus) 4m • 1.5t • Jur.
This plated dinosaur (p.44) was a gentle giant that spent most of the day munching plants. However, if *Huayangosaurus* was attacked, it was no more Mr Nice Guy! Its spines and plates went a scary scarlet, and its spiked tail could gouge a big hole in an attacker's leg.

# ◀ HYBODUS
(HIGH-bow-duss) 2.5m • 300kg • Tri./Jur.
Sharks have been among the deadliest sea predators for 400 million years. *Hybodus* lived throughout the dinosaur era and looked much like today's sharks. It used its speed and sharp teeth to snatch other sea creatures.

38

# HYLAEOSAURUS ▼

**(HIGH-lee-oh-SAW-rus) 4.5m • 5t • Cretaceous**

Like most armoured dinosaurs (p.10), *Hylaeosaurus* was a slow mover. With all those heavy armour plates weighing it down, it probably couldn't run faster than a slow trot! Scientists can tell how fast a dinosaur moved by looking at its fossilized tracks (p.72).

*Hylaeosaurus*' armour could be used for attack as well as defence: like many plant-eaters, males may have competed by looking fierce, roaring and then banging into each other! *Hylaeosaurus* was similar to *Polacanthus* and herds of these two dinosaurs often lived together.

## HYPSILOPHODON ▶

**(HIP-si-LOH-foh-don) 2.5m • 65kg • Cret.**

This ornithopod (p.29) lived in herds across Europe and North America. It nibbled low-lying plants and stored the leaves in its cheek pouches before chewing them with its back teeth. Running away was *Hypsilophodon's* only defence and it could dodge and weave like an antelope. It also had sharp eyes to spot approaching flesh-eaters.

# I

## ICHTHYOSAURUS ▼

**(IK-thee-oh-SAW-rus) 3m • 90kg • Jurassic**

If you crossed a dolphin with a shark, it might look like this sea-going reptile! A fast swimmer, *Ichthyosaurus* had big eyes for hunting fish and squid in deep, dark waters. Fossils show it gave birth to live young in the water, like a dolphin.

Rhamphorhynchus

Ichthyosaurus

## IGUANODON ▼
**(ig-WAH-noh-don) 8m • 4.5t • Cretaceous**
This famous ornithopod (p.29) roamed the woodlands of America and Europe in large herds. It usually walked and rested on all fours, but reared up to feed on tree ferns and conifer leaves. It ran from predators, but if cornered it would jab at them with its large spiked thumb.

## J

## JANENSCHIA ▼
**(yan-EN-shee-ah)**
**24m • 33t • Jurassic**
Like a giraffe, this sauropod (p.87) used its long neck to grab leaves from the tree tops. But it needed a very powerful heart to pump blood up to its brain. Otherwise lifting its head up high would have made it dizzy, even though it had a tiny brain!

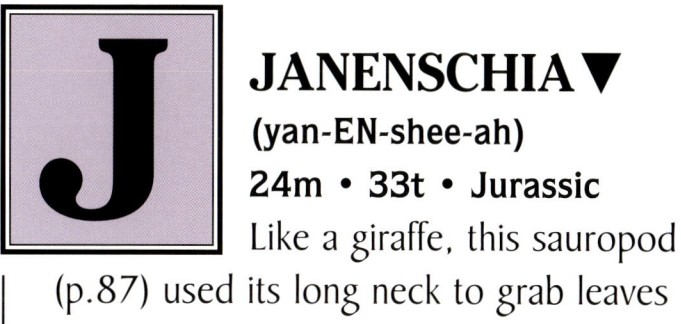

## INCISIVOSAURUS ▼
**(in-SIZE-ee-voh-SAW-rus) 1m • 20kg • Cret.**
This furry little dinosaur (p.13) had a parrot-like beak and big front teeth like a rabbit! Unlike most theropods (p.74), it was a plant-eater.

## JOBARIA ▼
**(joh-BARE-ee-uh) 23m • 20t • Cretaceous**
*Jobaria* was a massive plant-eater with a shorter tail than most sauropods (p.87). It lived in herds, browsing on thick vegetation in what is now North Africa. By looking at elephant behaviour, scientists have worked out that even a giant like *Jobaria* could stand on its hind legs to reach the tops of tall trees.

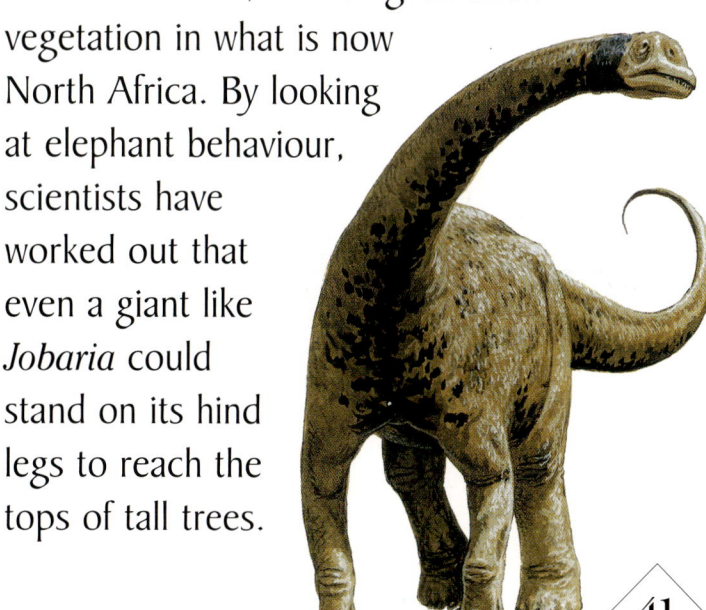

41

Pterodactylus
Mamenchisaurus
Megalosaurus
Apatosaurus
Heterodontosaurus
Ceratosaurus

# J

## JURASSIC PERIOD

Early dinosaurs living in the Triassic period were relatively small. However, in the Jurassic period, lasting from 205 to 144 million years ago, the real monsters appeared. The warm, wet Jurassic climate meant a plentiful and widespread supply of trees, ferns and horsetails to feed giant plant-eaters like *Apatosaurus* and *Mamenchisaurus*. Along with smaller plant-eaters such as *Heterodontosaurus* and *Tuojiangosaurus* they provided meals for increasingly big predators like *Yangchuanosaurus* and *Ceratosaurus*.

The Jurassic skies were dominated by skin-winged pterosaurs (p.60) such as *Pterodactylus*, although the first birds also appeared in this period. The seas and oceans were inhabited by dolphin-like ichthyosaurs and long-necked plesiosaurs.

Dilophosaurus

Yangchuanosaurus

Tuojiangosaurus

Archaeopteryx

Muraenosaurus

43

# K

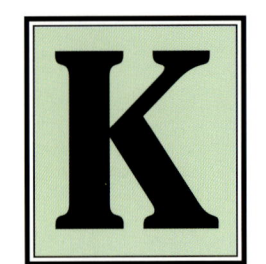

## KANNEMEYERIA ▼
(KAN-ah-may-uh-REE-ah)
2m • 150kg • Triassic

This stocky plant-eater was a dicynodont: a mammal-like reptile, not a dinosaur. A slow-moving creature with sprawling legs, it lived on the dry, dusty plains of what is now Africa. It was hunted by predators like *Cynognathus*.

## KRONOSAURUS ▼
(kron-oh-SAW-rus) 9m • 12t • Cretaceous

This giant sea predator had an enormous skull and 25cm-long teeth. Using its powerful flippers to push it through the water, it hunted plesiosaurs, fish and squid.

## KENTROSAURUS ▼
(KEN-troh-SAW-rus) 5.5m • 2t • Jur.

This stegosaur had long spines on its back, tail and sides. Like most plated dinosaurs it had a narrow mouth with big cheeks to stop its food falling out! It reared up on its long hind legs to reach leafy twigs.

### Plated dinosaurs

Stegosaurus — 8m long

The plated dinosaurs, or 'stegosaurs', were slow-moving, four-legged plant-eaters that grew up to 9m long. Each stegosaur had its own unique pattern of plates, spines and spikes.

Look out for these plated dinosaurs:
- Dacentrurus
- Huayangosaurus
- Kentrosaurus • Stegosaurus
- Tuojiangosaurus
- Wuerhosaurus

# L

## LAMBEOSAURUS ▶
(LAM-bee-oh-SAW-rus)
12m • 6t • Cretaceous

*Lambeosaurus* was one of the largest duckbill dinosaurs (p.82). It had a plate-shaped crest that could grow bigger than the rest of its head! It also had a narrow beak, so perhaps *Lambeosaurus* was a more fussy eater than other duckbills.

## LEEDSICHTHYS ▼
(leeds-IK-this) 30m • 40t • Jurassic

This was perhaps the biggest fish of all time. Like a blue whale, it swam with its mouth open to sift the water for plankton. A massive bony plate protected its head.

## LESOTHOSAURUS ▼
(le-SO-toh-SAW-rus) 1m • 3.5kg • Jur.

The size of a small deer, *Lesothosaurus* lived alongside *Heterodontosaurus* in the sandy scrub of South Africa. Like other ornithopods (p.29), it lived in big herds for protection. While some of the herd nibbled away with their heads down, others had their heads up to watch for predators. If a flesh-eater was spotted, this nimble animal had a good chance of escape.

45

Ichthyosaurus

# L

## LIOPLEURODON ▼

(lie-oh-PLOOR-oh-don) 19m • 50t • Jurassic

*Liopleurodon* was one of the most awesome flesh-eaters the world has ever seen. Like *Kronosaurus*, it belonged to a family of giant undersea reptiles called 'pliosaurs'. *Liopleurodon* had a skull as big as a car and teeth up to 25cm long. It used its flippers to 'fly' through the water and its huge jaws to crush fish, squid, ammonites, and ichthyosaurs, as well as dinosaurs that strayed too close to the water's edge. The discovery of a complete *Liopleurodon* skeleton in 2002 was the largest dinosaur ever found.

Ammonite

Liopleurodon

Mosasaurus

47

# M

## MACROPOMA ▶
(mak-roh-POH-ma)
60cm • 5kg • Cretaceous

*Macropoma* was a medium-sized fish with a short, deep body and large fins. This species of fish was thought to be extinct but its close relative, the *Coelacanth*, was rediscovered in 1938!

## Dinosaur young

Fossils show that baby dinosaurs had big heads, big eyes and short, little legs – just like human babies! Like birds, dinosaur young may have been covered in downy fur.

Fossils of trampled eggshells show that Maiasaura babies stayed in their nests for a long time after they were born, while adults cared for them. Like birds, Maiasauras carried food back to the nest for their young to eat. Most other young dinosaurs were probably left to fend for themselves after they hatched.

Maiasaura laid its eggs in a nest, while sauropod (p.87) eggs were laid in a straight line. Perhaps the giant plant-eaters laid them as they walked along.

## MAIASAURA ▶
(my-ah-SAW-rah) 9m • 4t • Cret.

A typical duckbill dinosaur (p.82), *Maiasaura* was a plant-eater with a tough beak, powerful jaws and small, horn-like crests above its eyes. Giant herds of *Maiasaura* trekked across North America, and each year the females returned to the same site, scooping out mud nests 2m across and laying up to 20 oval eggs.

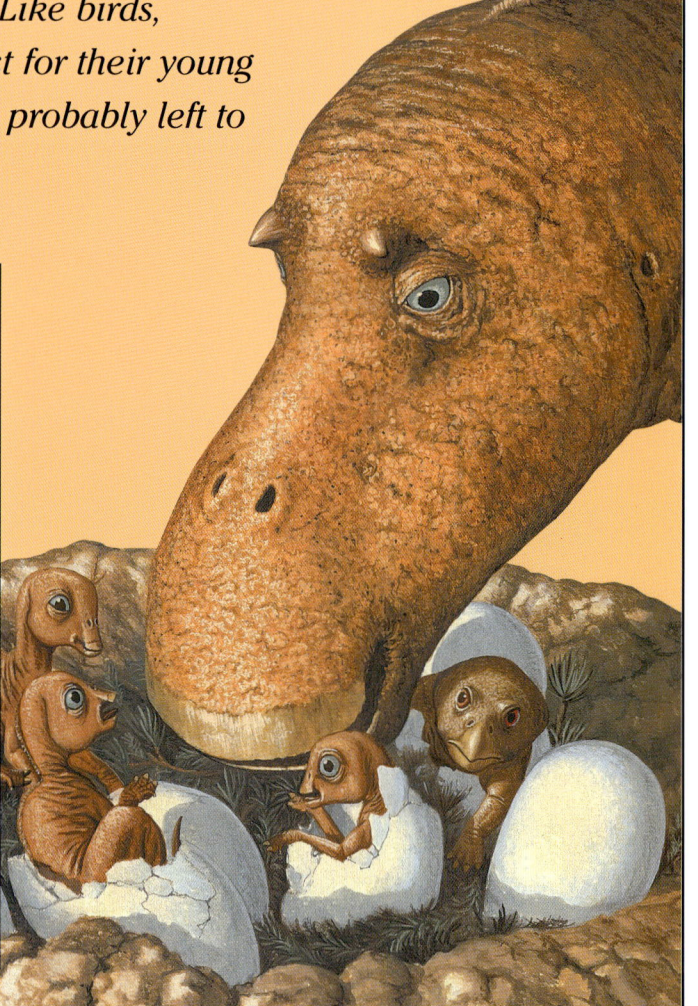

## ◀ MASIAKASAURUS
(MA-see-ah-ka-SAW-rus) 2m • 35kg • Cret.
This dog-sized theropod (p.74) had front teeth that stuck out like spears, probably for grabbing fish. Its species name, *knopfleri*, was named after Mark Knopfler from the 1980s rock band Dire Straits. Scientists who found the fossil were listening to his music when they dug it up!

## MAMENCHISAURUS ▼
(mah-MEN-chee-SAW-rus)
**22m • 27t • Jurassic**
This Chinese sauropod (p.87) had a neck 15m long, perhaps the longest neck ever! This allowed it to reach for food without moving the rest of its giant body. It lived in herds, where adults protected the young from predators like *Yangchuanosaurus*.

## MASSOSPONDYLUS ▲
(MAS-oh-SPON-die-lus) 6m • 500kg • Jur.
This common prosauropod (p.58) had a long neck and tail, a small head and big, grasping hands with a large thumb claw. It could run on two legs, and fossilised tracks show it was a fast runner for a prosauropod.

## MEGALOSAURUS ▲
(meg-ah-loh-SAW-rus) 8m • 1t • Jurassic
This heavy hunter (p.8) had a thick neck, short, strong arms, great curved fangs and fiendishly long claws on its feet. In 1824 it was the first dinosaur to be given a name, which we still use today.

## MEGARAPTOR ▼
(meg-ah-RAP-tor) 8m • 4t • Cretaceous
*Megaraptor* was a plant-eater's nightmare: large, fast-moving, agile and clever. It was equipped with razor-sharp teeth and claws on its hands and feet, including a 35cm talon on the second toe of each foot. Its claws were covered in a horny material like fingernails, making them even longer and sharper. Hunting in packs (p.25), it could kill almost anything it met.

## ◀ MEGAZOSTRODON
(meg-ah-ZOH-stroh-don) 10cm • 200g • Tri./Jur.
One of the earliest mammals, this tiny, shrew-like animal had a long tail and body and a long snout. Its sharp teeth were used for catching insects. Like small mammals today, it hunted at night when most birds and reptiles were resting.

# MELANOROSAURUS ▶

(MEL-an-OR-oh-SAW-rus) 12m • 8t • Tri.

This African prosauropod (p.58) had heavy bones, a bulky body with a long tail and a small head at the end of a long neck. Like many prosauropods, its rear legs were longer than its front legs.

# ◀ METRIORHYNCHUS

(MET-ree-oh-RINK-us) 3m • 250kg • Jur.

This sea-going reptile looked like a crocodile with its webbed feet, but it had a tail more like a fish. Its slim jaws had rows of teeth perfect for catching slippery fish, and like a crocodile it would come ashore to lay eggs or bask in the sun.

## Bonehead dinosaurs

This group of medium-sized plant-eaters had bird-shaped hips (p.34) and lived in herds like their horned relatives (p.19). They are famous for their heavy skulls which were up to 25cm thick. Males may have used them in head-butting fights during the breeding season, like wild goats today.

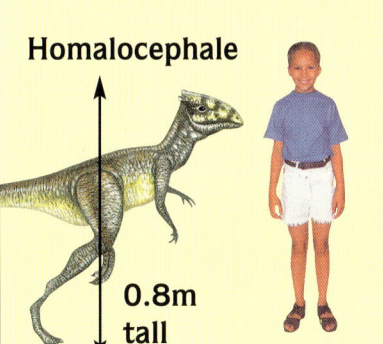

Homalocephale
0.8m tall

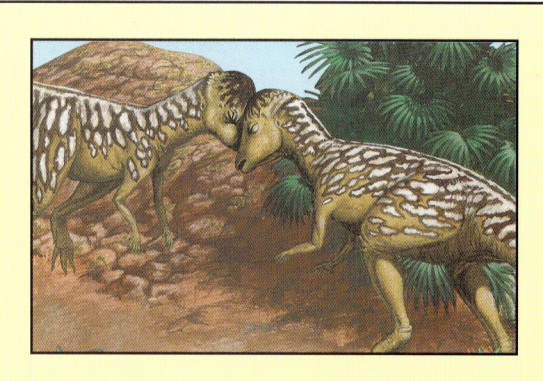

**Look out for these boneheads:**
- Homalocephale
- Micropachycephalosaurus
- Stegoceras • Wannanosaurus
- Yaverlandia

# MICROPACHYCEPHALOSAURUS

(my-kroh-pak-ee-SEF-ah-loh-SAW-rus) 0.5m • 15kg • Cret.

*Micropachycephalosaurus* is one of the smallest dinosaurs so far discovered, but has the longest dinosaur name! This little boneheaded plant-eater was found in China.

51

## MICRORAPTOR ▶
**(my-kroh-RAP-tor) 0.5m • 10kg • Cret.**
The smallest dinosaur yet found, this theropod (p.74) was covered in fine hairs, and feathers sprouted from its arms. It was a good climber and hunted in the trees. In 2003, fossils of a new species – *Microraptor gui* – were discovered China. It had four wing-like limbs and is a vital link between dinosaurs and birds.

## MINMI ▲
**(min-MEE) 3m • 2t • Cretaceous**
*Minmi* is the dinosaur with the shortest name, and the first dinosaur found in Australia. Like *Edmontonia*, it was an armoured dinosaur (p.10) without a bony club on its tail. Small bony plates protected its stomach, and thorny plates ran along its tail. This group of dinosaurs were called 'nodosaurids'.

## MONONYKUS ▼
**(mon-oh-NIE-kus) 1m • 20kg • Cret.**
This turkey-sized theropod (p.74) had stubby little arms, each with a single claw. Scientists cannot agree whether it was a flightless bird or a feathered dinosaur (p.13) that used its arms to burrow into the ground.

Mononykus long legs made it a quick runner.

# MOSASAURUS ▲

**(moh-zah-SAW-rus) 10m • 13t • Cret.**
Mosasaurs were a group of reptiles living in the shallow Cretaceous oceans. Growing up to 10m long, they were among the biggest predators ever. Like other mosasaurs such as *Tylosaurus*, *Mosasaurus* preyed on large fish, turtles and plesiosaurs. It swam by moving its long, flexible tail from side to side while steering with its flippers.

# MUSSAURUS ▼

**(mus-SAW-rus) 10cm • 2kg • Triassic**
Called 'mouse lizard', this tiny dinosaur is perhaps a baby *Plateosaurus* (p.58) rather than a new species. Though only a few centimetres long, it could have grown into a dinosaur weighing 120kg or more.

# ◄ MUTTABURRASAURUS

**(MUT-ah-BUR-ah-SAW-rus)**
**7m • 3.5t • Cretaceous**
This large ornithopod (p.29) may have migrated to the South Pole each summer. In the Cretaceous period there was no ice at the poles, but large forests full of food for a hungry *Muttaburrasaurus*. Its hands were built for stripping leaves, and it had spiked thumbs like *Iguanodon*.

# N

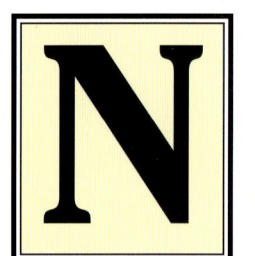

## NEMEGTOSAURUS ▶
**(ne-MEG-toh-SAW-rus) 21m • 20t • Cret.**
Only the sloping skull of this Asian sauropod (p.87) has been discovered. Scientists think it is a 'titanosaur' like *Saltasaurus*, a group of sauropods that survived late into the Cretaceous period.

## ◀ NOASAURUS
**(noh-ah-SAW-rus) 2m • 15kg • Cretaceous**
*Noasaurus* was a small South American theropod that lived alongside monster munchers like *Carnotaurus*. Though similar to pack hunters (p.25) like *Velociraptor*, it had an unusual foot claw.

## NODOSAURUS ▲
**(NODE-oh-SAW-rus) 5m • 3t • Cret.**
This plant-eater was an armoured dinosaur (p.10) without a bony club on its tail. Its name means 'knobbly lizard' after the bumpy plates on its back and sides.

## ▲ NOTHOSAURUS
**(noh-thoh-SAW-rus) 3m • 400kg • Tri.**
*Nothosaurus* was a long-necked, ocean-going predator with webbed feet and a long, flexible tail. Like a crocodile, it hunted in the water but rested and laid its eggs on land.

# O

### ORNITHOMIMUS
(OR-ni-thoh-MEE-mus) ▶
3.5m • 140kg • Cretaceous

Like most 'ostrich' dinosaurs (p.72), *Ornithomimus* ate meat *and* veg. It roamed the open countryside, pecking at plants and snapping up small animals with its beak. It could give a nasty kick with its toe claws, but it relied on its speed to escape from danger.

### ORNITHOSUCHUS ▲
(OR-ni-thoh-SOOK-us) 2m • 70kg • Triassic

This ancient reptile (p.64) looked like a crocodile. Though it could walk on its hind legs it probably spent most of the day on all fours. This medium-sized predator lived at the same time as the first dinosaurs.

### OVIRAPTOR ▼
(OH-vi-RAP-tor) 1.5m • 36kg • Cret.

*Oviraptor*'s name means 'egg thief', because the scientists who first found it believed it had been killed while stealing eggs from a *Protoceratops*' nest. Recent finds show that, in fact, these adult *Oviraptors* had died while protecting their own nests. Apart from its toothless beak, the rest of an *Oviraptor*'s body was like most theropods (p.74), with strong arms, long legs and a long, stiff tail.

Oviraptor egg

55

56

# P

## PARASAUROLOPHUS ▼
(par-ah-SAW-roh-LOAF-us)

10m • 7t • Cretaceous

Walking through a steamy Cretaceous swamp, the first thing you would have noticed about this duckbill dinosaur (p.82) was the bony crest on the top of its head. This was up to 1.8m long and *Parasaurolophus* may have used it to make low, foghorn-like sounds.

Like other duckbills, *Parasaurolophus* had no defence other than its size, so it lived in herds, relying on its large eyes, good hearing and good sense of smell to detect flesh-eaters lurking nearby.

## ◀ PELECANIMIMUS

(PEL-ee-can-ee-MEEM-us) 4m • 200kg • Cretaceous

This 'ostrich' dinosaur (p.72) had 220 tiny teeth in its jaws, more than any other theropod (p.74). These may have helped it to catch slippery fish in shallow lakes. Like a pelican, it had a skin pouch in its throat where it could store fish until it returned to the nest to feed its young.

## *Prosauropods:* early giants

The prosauropods of the late Triassic period were the first animals tall enough to eat from the trees. They used their muscular tongue or strong hands to grasp leaves. Though they could not chew their food, prosauropods swallowed pebbles, called gastroliths, which sat in their stomach and ground the tougher plants to a pulp. Prosauropods walked on all fours most of the time, but reared up on their hind legs to feed.

Riojasaurus — 5m tall

**Look out for these prosauropods:**
- Massospondylus • Melanorosaurus
- Mussaurus • Plateosaurus
- Riojasaurus • Thecodontosaurus

## ◀ PLATEOSAURUS

(plat-ee-oh-SAW-rus) 8m • 2t • Tri.

This well-known prosauropod had a bulky body and a long neck. It only had small teeth, so it used its thumb claws to rip off leaves and stuff them into its mouth with its five-fingered hands.

## POLACANTHUS ▲
(pole-ah-KAN-thus) 4m • 2t • Cretaceous
This armoured plant-eater (p.10) was very slow, but as it was protected by plates and spines it didn't need to run fast! It lived in mixed herds with *Hylaeosaurus*.

## PROTOCERATOPS ▼
(PRO-toh-SER-ah-tops) 1.8m • 400kg • Cret.
This small horned dinosaur (p.19) lived in a hot, dusty region of Mongolia, slicing tough, dry plants with it's hard beak and strong jaws. Fossils show that it lived in big families and nested in the sand dunes.

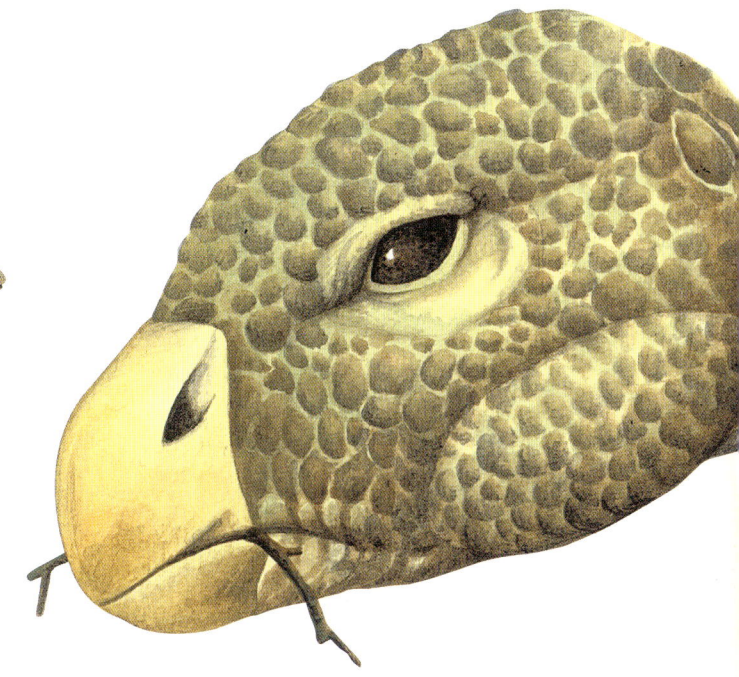

## PSITTACOSAURUS ▲
(si-TAK-oh-SAW-rus) 2m • 50kg • Cret.
With its big jaws and parrot-like beak, this hardy little dinosaur chewed up palm tree trunks that were too tough for most plant-eaters. It also swallowed stones to grind up food in its stomach. Although it had no horns, it was related to larger horned dinosaurs (p.19).

# Flying reptiles

Flying reptiles, or 'pterosaurs', were close relatives of the dinosaurs. Their wings were made of a large flap of skin stretched over the equivalent of a very wide hand. Some pterosaurs had furry bodies and were warm-blooded, like mammals. Early pterosaurs were 1m to 3m across, but in the Cretaceous period, monsters with a wingspan of 10m or more appeared!

Quetzalcoatlus

Thalassodromeus

Anurognathus

1.3m

**Look out for these flying reptiles:**
- Anurognathus • Dimorphodon
- Dsungaripterus • Pteranodon
- Pterodactylus • Pterodaustro
- Quetzalcoatlus • Rhamphorhynchus
- Thalassodromeus • Tropeognathus

Pterosaurs walked awkwardly on all fours.

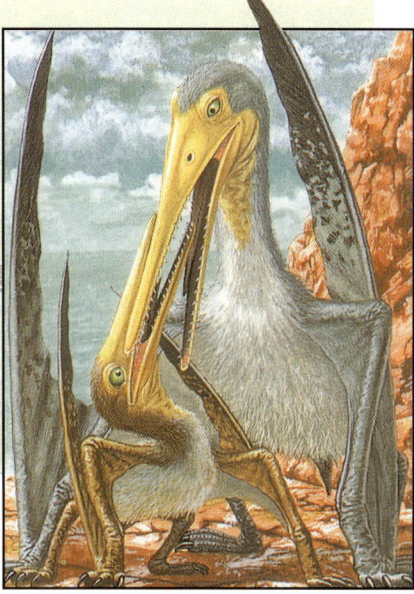

### ◀ PTERANODON

(ter-AN-oh-don) 8m across • 20kg • Cret.
This flying reptile had a large headcrest. In males this may have been brightly coloured to attract females. *Pteranodon* also had a pouch under its toothless bill to store fish which it caught. Like most big pterosaurs, it flew slowly but could turn quickly in the air. It took off from cliffs or trees and may have landed with a bump!

### PTERODACTYLUS ▲

(TER-oh-DAK-til-us) 1m across • 5kg • Jur.
*Pterodactylus* was a small pterosaur that hunted fish using its long, toothed beak. Recent finds show that it looked after its young like a bird, perhaps building a nest on the tops of trees or cliffs. On the ground it would be easy prey for a fast-moving flesh-eater.

### ◀ PTERODAUSTRO

(TER-oh-DOW-stroh) 4m across • 15kg • Cret.
This pterosaur had long jaws that curved upward and contained up to a thousand teeth! These made its mouth like a sieve, so *Pterodaustro* could strain beakfuls of water, trapping plankton and other small sea creatures inside. It may have trailed its jaws in the water as it skimmed along the surface.

## QUETZALCOATLUS ▲

(KWET-sal-koh-AT-lus) 12m across • 26kg • Cret.

*Quetzalcoatlus* was the biggest pterosaur (p.60) of all, with a wingspan of 11-12m. That's three times the size of the biggest bird and more like a small aeroplane!

When *Quetzalcoatlus* was first discovered, scientists thought it fed on rotting carcasses like a vulture. But the shape of its neck shows that it probably ate fish and other small animals it picked up from the surface of the water. It may have migrated hundreds of kilometres to and from its breeding grounds.

## R RHAMPHORHYNCHUS ▼

**(RAM-foh-RINK-us) 2m across • 20kg • Jur.**

Like *Pterodactylus*, this pterosaur (p.60) hunted for fish, skimming over the waves, then plunging its bill into the water to snatch up prey. Its sharp, pointed teeth were perfect for grasping a wriggling fish.

## RIOJASAURUS ▼

**(ree-OH-ah-SAW-rus) 11m • 4.5t • Triassic**

*Riojasaurus* was one of the largest prosauropods (p.58). It needed to eat a massive amount to stay alive, so its big gut was stuffed with heavy plant food, forcing it to walk on all fours like the giant sauropods (p.87). It was just too big for most Triassic predators to risk attacking. It also had a long, powerful tail which could kill a small flesh-eater like *Coelophysis* with a single blow.

# S

## SALTASAURUS ▶

(sal-tah-SAW-rus) 12m • 7t • Cret.

*Saltasaurus* was small for a sauropod (p.87), but it was tough! It was covered in bony bumps and thick, round plates about the size of a human fist. Any attacker jumping on its back would have broken its teeth biting through this rock-hard skin. *Saltasaurus* also rocked back onto its hind legs to crush an attacker, using its tail for support.

## SALTOPOSUCHUS

(SALT-oh-poh-SOOK-us) 1m • 50kg • Tri.

This archosaur was a flesh-eater with sharp, pointed teeth and two rows of armoured plates on its back. It had long back legs and short front legs. Its name means 'leaping crocodile'.

## Archosaurs: ruling reptiles

Archosaur means 'ruling lizard' and describes all the prehistoric reptiles that first appeared in the Triassic period, including dinosaurs, crocodiles, pterosaurs and marine reptiles.

**Look out for these archosaurs:**
- *All dinosaurs* • *All flying reptiles (p.60)*
- *Ornithosuchus* • *Saltoposuchus*
- *Sarcosuchus* • *Sharovipteryx*

Sarcosuchus grabs a Hypsilophodon.

# SARCOSUCHUS ▼
(sar-koh-SOOK-us) 13m • 10t • Cretaceous

Crocodiles appeared about the same time as dinosaurs. This monstrous archosaur (p.64) was bigger than *T. rex*! Its body was covered in thick armour and there were over 100 teeth in its long jaws. It ambushed prey by lying still before leaping out of the water.

# SAUROLOPHUS ▼
(SAW-roh-LOW-fus) 10m • 9t • Cret.

This duckbill dinosaur (p.82) had a bony spike sticking up from the top of its forehead. This may have been attached to a flap of skin covering the nostrils, that could be used to make loud noises in defence, or by males to attract females.

# SAUROPELTA ▼
(SAW-roh-PEL-tah) 7m • 3t • Cret.

This wide armoured plant-eater (p.10) was covered in rows of bony cones and studs and had bony spikes jutting from its sides. Its broad mouth would have gobbled down most plants, including flowering plants such as roses, vines and magnolias that first appeared during the Cretaceous period.

# SAURORNITHOIDES ▼
(saw-ROR-nith-OID-eez) 2m • 60kg • Cret.
*Saurornithoides* was a flat-footed theropod (p.74) that hunted lizards and other small animals. Its skull had space for a big brain so it was probably clever for a dinosaur.

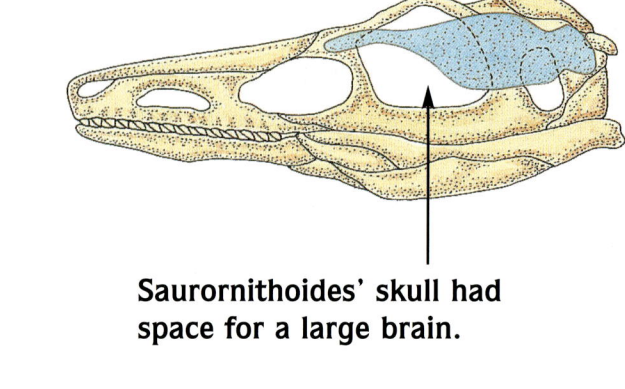

**Saurornithoides' skull had space for a large brain.**

# SCELIDOSAURUS ▼
(skel-IDE-oh-SAW-rus) 4m • 400kg • Jur.
About the size of a small car, *Scelidosaurus* was one of the earliest armoured dinosaurs (p.10). It had a long body with seven rows of bony spines running along its back. If cornered by an attacker, it crouched down to protect its soft belly.

# SEGNOSAURUS ▶
(SEG-noh-SAW-rus) 6.5m • 2t • Cret.
*Segnosaurus* was a therizinosaur (p.77), a strange theropod with scythe-shaped claws. It was a slow-moving, flat-footed creature that walked on its hind legs. Its claws were not suited to tearing flesh, so it probably ate plants or insects. *Segnosaurus* fossils have been found in Mongolia.

# ◀ SHAROVIPTERYX
(shah-rov-IP-terr-iks) 50cm • 3kg • Tri.
This bizarre-looking early reptile (p.64) had a flap of skin stretched between its front and back legs. It couldn't fly but used its 'wings' to glide from tree to tree like a modern flying lizard. It might have been an ancestor of the pterosaurs (p.60).

# SIDEROPS ▶
(side-eh-ROPS) 2.5m • 150kg • Jur.
This Australian amphibian had a large, wide head, sharp teeth, and curved tusks. Though it mainly hunted freshwater fish and frogs, it was strong enough to grab small dinosaurs from the water's edge.

### ◀ SINORNIS

(si-NOR-nis) 10cm • 100g • Cret.

This sparrow-sized bird was discovered in China. It was a much better flier than the earliest birds (like *Archaeopteryx*). It had a toothed beak suitable for catching small insects while in flight. By the end of the Cretaceous period, birds like *Sinornis* had already begun to take over from the skin-winged pterosaurs (p.60) as masters of the skies.

### SINOSAUROPTERYX ▼

(SIGH-noh-saw-ROP-ter-iks) 1m • 15kg • Jur.

*Sinosauropteryx* was the first dinosaur fossil ever found covered with feathers like a bird (p.13). Since it couldn't fly, it probably had feathers to keep it warm. A fast theropod (p.74) with a very long tail, it is also the only dinosaur fossil that has been found with a mammal in its stomach.

**Sinosauropteryx feathers**

## SPINOSAURUS ▼
(SPY-noh-SAW-rus)

12m • 6t • Cretaceous

As long and as heavy as *T. rex*, *Spinosaurus* was an odd-looking theropod (p.74) with crocodile-like jaws and narrow pointed teeth for catching fish. The 1.6m-tall skin 'sail' on its back may have helped it to warm up in the sun.

## *Dinosaur body heat*

*Scientists aren't sure whether dinosaurs warmed up or cooled down as the air temperature changed during the day. Big dinosaurs may have kept warm just by being big, while dinosaurs with small bodies may have been warm-blooded, like mammals. Some dinosaurs, such as Stegosaurus (above), could pump blood into plates or sails to warm up quickly in the sun or cool down in the shade.*

## ◀ STEGOCERAS
(steg-oh-SER-ass) 2.5m • 50kg • Cret.

*Stegoceras* was a bonehead dinosaur (p.51) about the size of a goat (but with a long tail). Its heavy skull got thicker and higher as it grew older, and males probably tussled head-to-head in fights to win females. It was a fairly slow-moving dinosaur that tilted forward as it moved, using its stiff, heavy tail to balance the weight of its large, domed head.

69

# S

## STEGOSAURUS
**(STEG-oh-SAW-rus) 8m • 3t • Jurassic**

*Stegosaurus* was the biggest plated dinosaur (p.44), with a row of broad, flat plates down its back. The large blood vessels in these plates helped it to warm up and cool down (p.69) and *Stegosaurus* could turn the plates bright red if it needed to scare off predators or rivals in its herd.

*Stegosaurus* had a top speed of 20kph, so it relied on its size and armour rather than speed for protection – it lashed out at predators using its spiky tail. It had a small head and a narrow beak without teeth, suited to eating only soft leaves or flowers. Inside its skull was a brain the size of a walnut, so *Stegosaurus* was not the cleverest dinosaur in the forest!

71

# STEROPODON ▶

**(ster-OH-poh-don) 35cm • 200g • Cretaceous**

Though only the size of a small cat, *Steropodon* was one of the biggest mammals of the dinosaur era. Like its living relative, the platypus, it laid eggs and hunted small animals in freshwater creeks. Its legs stuck out at the sides like early reptiles and crocodiles.

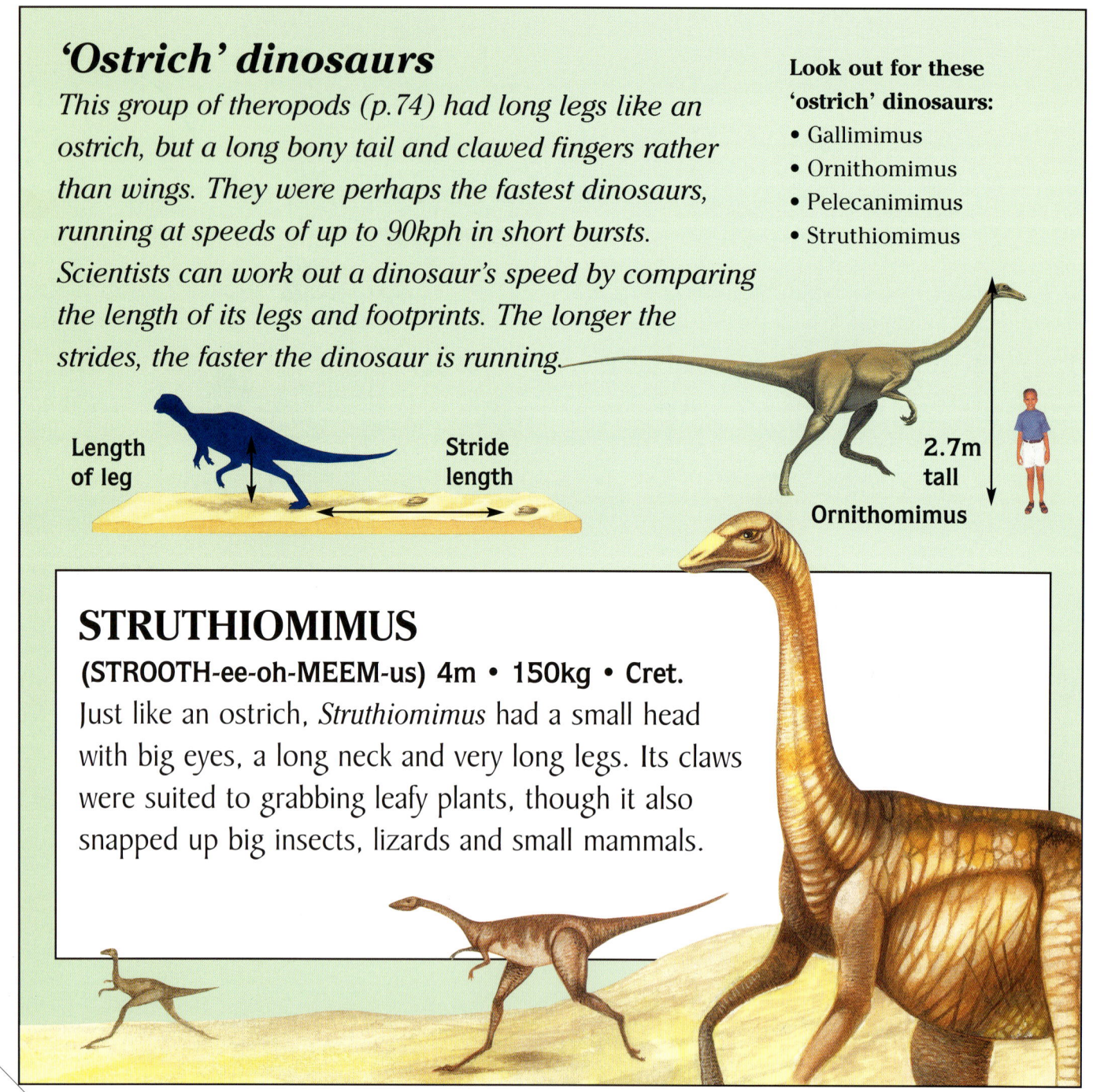

## 'Ostrich' dinosaurs

This group of theropods (p.74) had long legs like an ostrich, but a long bony tail and clawed fingers rather than wings. They were perhaps the fastest dinosaurs, running at speeds of up to 90kph in short bursts. Scientists can work out a dinosaur's speed by comparing the length of its legs and footprints. The longer the strides, the faster the dinosaur is running.

Look out for these 'ostrich' dinosaurs:
- Gallimimus
- Ornithomimus
- Pelecanimimus
- Struthiomimus

Length of leg

Stride length

Ornithomimus — 2.7m tall

## STRUTHIOMIMUS

**(STROOTH-ee-oh-MEEM-us) 4m • 150kg • Cret.**

Just like an ostrich, *Struthiomimus* had a small head with big eyes, a long neck and very long legs. Its claws were suited to grabbing leafy plants, though it also snapped up big insects, lizards and small mammals.

## STYRACOSAURUS ▶
**(sty-RAK-oh-SAW-rus) 5.5m • 3t • Cret.**
This horned plant-eater (p.19) had six spikes sticking out from its bony neck frill. The biggest of these were about as long as a man's arm. This frill would have protected its neck from attack by large predators. Scars found on *Styracosaurus* fossils show the frills were also used in shoving contests with rival males.

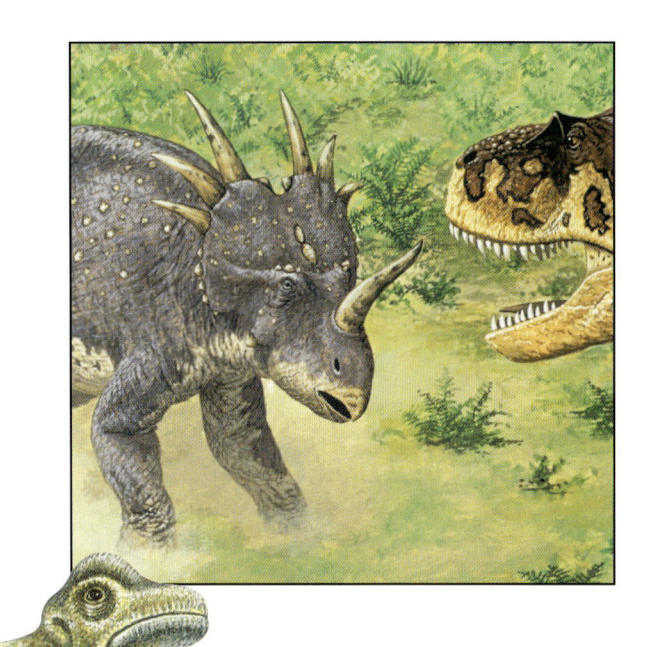

## ◀ SUPERSAURUS
**(soo-per-SAW-rus) 42m • 55t • Jur.**
A member of the sauropod group (p.87), *Supersaurus* is one of the longest animals to have ever lived on land. Although it had a 12m-long neck, *Supersaurus* could not lift its head up very high. It may have stood on solid ground and stretched its neck out to reach soft plants in marshy areas. Its blunt teeth were perfect for stripping fern or conifer leaves. Because it swallowed leaves whole, it probably had stones in its stomach to grind up the toughest parts.

## SYNTARSUS ▶
**(sin-TAR-sus) 3m • 30kg • Tri./Jur.**
*Syntarsus* was a nimble, fast-moving theropod (p.74) with a long neck and a long pointed head. It lived in a dry, semi-desert region where it hunted in packs. A gang of these small flesh-eaters could overwhelm a much larger animal: the remains of 30 *Syntarsus* skeletons were found in one fossil site next to a 250kg *Massospondylus*.

# T

## TALARURUS ▼
(tal-ah-ROO-rus) 6m • 6t • Cret.
*Talarurus* was an armoured dinosaur (p.10) like *Euoplocephalus*, with bony spines and a bony club at the end of its tail. With all its armoured parts, *Talarurus* had about 700 bones – that's 500 more than a human!

## TANYSTROPHEUS ▼
(TAN-ee-STRO-fee-us) 3m • 500kg • Tri.
This bizarre reptile had a neck twice the length of its body. Like today's geckos, it also had a special tail which snapped off if grabbed by an attacker, allowing it to run away. *Tanystropheus* wasn't a very good swimmer or runner, so it may have hunted from the water's edge, snapping at fish and grabbing them with its sharp teeth.

Tanystropheus had four feet and possibly webbed toes.

## TARBOSAURUS ▶
(TAR-boh-SAW-rus) 10m • 1.5t • Cret.
*Tarbosaurus* was a heavy hunter (p.8) like *T. rex* – so like it, in fact, that some scientists think it is a *T. rex*! It hunted *Saurolophus* and other duckbill dinosaurs (p.82) in what is now Mongolia. Armed with 15cm teeth and giant claws on its feet, it was the biggest theropod in the region.

## Theropods
This major group of lizard-hipped dinosaurs (p.34) appeared in the Triassic period and lasted through the Cretaceous. They had two strong legs with bird-like, clawed feet, and most were fast and agile. Almost all theropods were flesh-eaters with grasping hands, clawed fingers, sharp teeth or beaks and strong jaws. Many were clever dinosaurs with sharp senses (p.81). Some hunted in packs (p.25) and some were covered in feathers (p.13).

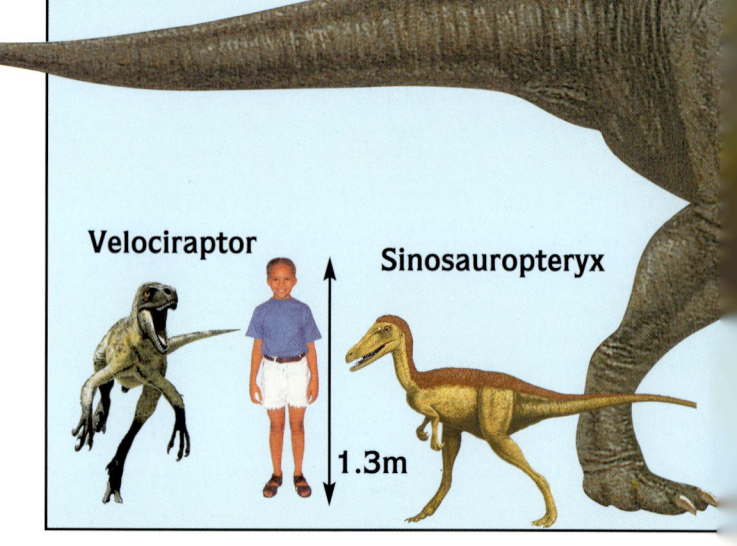

Velociraptor

Sinosauropteryx

1.3m

## TENONTOSAURUS ▼
(te-NON-toh-SAW-rus) 7m • 2t • Cret.
*Tenontosaurus* was a large ornithopod (p.29) that spent most of its time on all fours, grazing in lush swamps in what is now western North America. To escape from danger it ran on its two hind legs, which were slightly longer than its front legs.

## THALASSODROMEUS ▼
(tha-LASS-oh-DROH-mee-us)
4.5m across • 15kg • Cretaceous
This big pterosaur (p.60) had a head crowned by a huge, bony crest shaped like a spear. It snapped up fish with a scissor-like beak, as it skimmed over the water with its jaw trailing under the surface.

**Look out for these theropods:**
- *All heavy hunters (p.8)*
- *All therizinosaurs (p.77)*
- *All pack hunters (p.25)*
- *All feathered theropods (p.13) and birds (p.91)*
- *All 'ostrich' dinosaurs (p.72)*
- Afrovenator • Albertosaurus • Baryonyx
- Cryolophosaurus • Eoraptor • Gallimimus
- Gasosaurus • Giganotosaurus • Herrerasaurus
- Masiakasaurus • Oviraptor • Saurornithoides
- Sinosauropteryx • Spinosaurus • Syntarsus
- Tarbosaurus • Unenlagia • Velociraptor

**Giganotosaurus**

**Gallimimus**

**Eoraptor**

75

## THECODONTOSAURUS ▲

**(THEE-koh-DONT-oh-SAW-rus) 3m • 100kg • Tri.**

*Thecodontosaurus* is the earliest known prosauropod (p.58). Its fossils have been found in Britain, which was probably a dry desert during the Triassic period. It had a small head, long legs, thumb claws and a long tail. It walked on all fours, but ran on two legs.

Thecodontosaurus lived in family groups with its young.

## THERIZINOSAURUS

**(THER-ih-ZEEN-oh-SAW-rus)**

**11m • 5t • Cretaceous**

Like a modern gorilla, this gentle giant was suited to life in the forest. It ambled around on its massive hind limbs, stripping leaves with its long, clawed hands or reaching up with its flexible neck to strip leafy twigs with its toothless beak.

# TOROSAURUS ▼

**(TOR-oh-SAW-rus) 8m • 6t • Cret.**

*Torosaurus* was one of the largest horned dinosaurs (p.19). It had a stocky body, with a massive skull almost 3m long. Its neck was protected by a bony frill, and it had three horns: a short nose horn and two large brow horns. Despite its fierce looks, it spent most of the day nibbling on plants, like other horned dinosaurs.

# THESCELOSAURUS ▲

**(thes-KEL-oh-SAW-rus) 3.5m • 1.5t • Cret.**

*Thescelosaurus* was an ornithopod (p.29) with a small head, a bulky body, a long tail and short arms. When scientists dug up this dinosaur in 2000, they found a fossilized heart which showed that some dinosaurs may have have been warm-blooded creatures (p.69).

## *Therizinosaurs*

This family of weird and wonderful theropods (p.74) had toothless beaks, long scythe-like claws, and four-toed feet like a prosauropod. Scientists worked out what therizinosaurs looked like by combining parts from different species within the family. The latest finds show they may have been covered with fine feathers, like an emu.

Alxasaurus

4m long

Alxasaurus claw

**Look out for these therizinosaurs:**
- Alxasaurus
- Erlikosaurus
- Segnosaurus
- Therizinosaurus

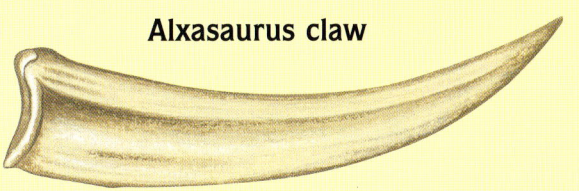

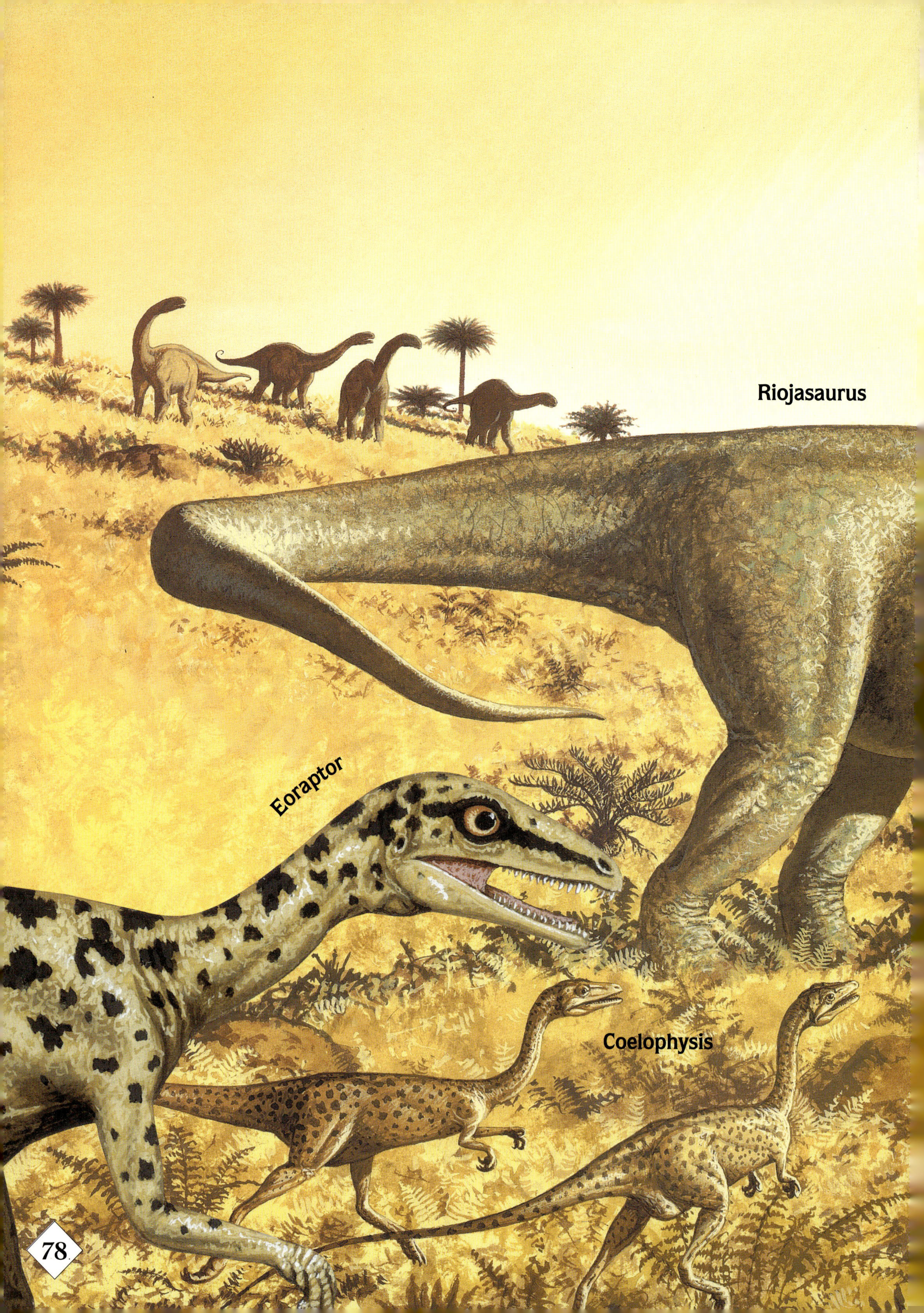
Riojasaurus
Eoraptor
Coelophysis

## T

## TRIASSIC PERIOD

During the Triassic period, which lasted from 250 to 205 million years ago, all the land was in one giant continent, called Pangaea, and the climate was generally warm. Conifer trees, palm-like cycads, and ferns grew in wet areas, although there were many desert regions. At first, cynodonts, primitive dinosaurs, and other ancient reptiles ruled the land, but they were eventually wiped out in two mass extinctions. They were replaced by new dinosaurs: giant plant-eaters like *Riojasaurus* and agile hunters like *Coelophysis*. Pterosaurs (p.60) also developed from winged reptiles like *Sharovipteryx*.

Syntarsus

79

## TRICERATOPS ▲
**(try-SER-ah-tops)**
**8m • 6t • Cretaceous**

*Triceratops* is the most famous horned dinosaur (p.19). As heavy as two elephants, it had three horns and its neck was protected by a broad, bony frill sticking out from the back of its head. This frill may have helped it to warm up and cool down like the plates on *Stegosaurus* (p.69). Old wounds in *Triceratops* skulls show that males locked horns when they fought each other.

## TRILOPHOSAURUS ▲
**(try-LOAF-oh-SAW-rus) 3m • 400kg • Triassic**

This plant-eating reptile had a heavily-built skull with a narrow snout and broad, flat teeth perfect for chomping up tough plants like woody ferns. It also had a long, heavy tail.

### ◀ TROODON

**(TROO-oh-don) 2m • 50kg • Cret.**
This human-sized pack-hunter (p.25) was one of the most intelligent dinosaurs. It was armed with hook-like claws on its hands and feet, including a deep, curved claw on its second toe. Its large eyes allowed it to hunt at dusk, when small mammals came out to feed, though it also hunted lizards and young dinosaurs.

## Dinosaur brains

In the past, dinosaurs were seen as just plain stupid. Today, scientists can work out roughly how intelligent a dinosaur was by comparing its brain size to its body size. Most plant-eaters probably were very stupid – Stegosaurus had a brain the size of a walnut! However, small pack hunters (p.25) like Troodon needed bigger brains to hunt together and were as clever as birds today.

Most flesh-eaters relied on large eyes and sensitive noses or ears to hunt their prey. To control these organs, they needed a large brain. However, because the ornithopod Leaellynasaura (lee-el-in-na-SAW-ra) (below) lived near the South Pole, it also had big eyes to search for food in the constant night of the winter months.

### ◀ TROPEOGNATHUS

**(TRO-pee-og-NAY-thus) 6m across • 20kg • Cret.**
This large pterosaur (p.60) was found in Brazil. It had a short tail and wide wings suited to gliding. It lived near the sea and hunted fish, snapping them up in its toothy beak.

81

## Duckbill dinosaurs

The duckbill dinosaurs, or 'hadrosaurs', are named after their beak-like mouths. Up to 15m long, they replaced the sauropods (p.87) as the most successful large plant-eaters. They had amazing crests with long tubes inside linking the nostrils to the throat. When a hadrosaur breathed out it could make a low noise like a trumpet. Different hadrosaurs had different-shaped crests, so each species made its own sound.

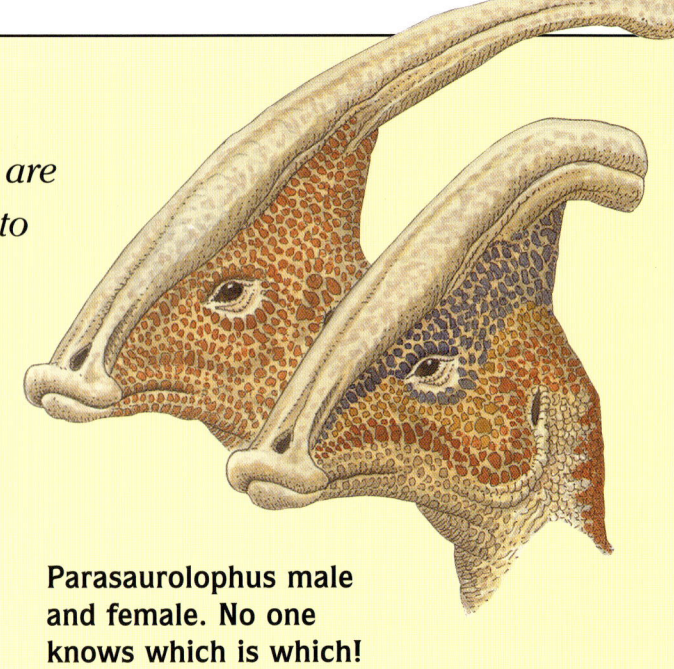

**Parasaurolophus male and female. No one knows which is which!**

**Look out for these duckbill dinosaurs:**
- Corythosaurus
- Edmontosaurus
- Lambeosaurus
- Maiasaura
- Parasaurolophus
- Saurolophus
- Tsintaosaurus

All duckbills are ornithopods (p.29)

4.5m tall

**Maiasaura**

### ◀ TSINTAOSAURUS

(SIN-tau-SAW-rus) 10m • 9t • Cret.
The remains of this mysterious duckbill dinosaur were found in China. The thin, hollow crest on its head may have been used to make low sounds, like the crest on *Parasaurolophus* (above). Like all duckbills, it probably had fleshy pads on its four-fingered hands, making it easier to walk on all fours.

## TUOJIANGOSAURUS ▲
(toh-wang-oh-SAW-rus) 9m • 3t • Jur.
This plated dinosaur (p.44) from China had a high humped back and a long, heavy tail. Two rows of up to 15 bony plates ran along its back and tail, and two pairs of spikes stuck out from the end of its tail. *Tuojiangosaurus* had a small head with a small jaw and large cheeks. Like all stegosaurs (p.44) it had to eat huge amounts of plant food to keep its big body going.

## TYLOSAURUS ▼
(tie-loh-SAW-rus) 12m • 10t • Cret.
*Tylosaurus* was a 'mosasaur', a flesh-eating marine reptile. It was a powerful swimmer that had four paddle-like limbs on a long, streamlined body. It had large jaws with rows of sharp teeth.

**Tylosaurus hunted fish, turtles and long-necked plesiosaurs.**

# TYRANNOSAURUS REX ▲

**(tie-RAN-oh-SAW-rus-REKS) 12m • 7t • Cretaceous**

The most famous dinosaur of them all, *Tyrannosaurus rex*, or *T. rex* for short, was perhaps the most powerful flesh-eater ever to walk on Earth. This heavy hunter (p.8) weighed more than an elephant. With massive jaws and 18cm-long teeth, *T. rex* was a deadly enemy. It ambushed live prey by rushing forward with its jaws wide open.

 *T. rex's* big clawed feet pinned its prey down while it tore off chunks of flesh with its mouth. Scientists are unsure how it used its tiny arms, but one theory is that *T. rex* hooked them into its prey to hold it still.

85

# U

Ultrasauros protected their young by living in herds.

Diplodocus

6m tall

**Look out for these sauropods:**
- Amargasaurus • Antarctosaurus
- Apatosaurus • Barosaurus
- Brachiosaurus • Camarasaurus
- Cetiosaurus • Diplodocus
- Janenschia • Jobaria
- Mamenchisaurus
- Nemegtosaurus • Saltasaurus
- Supersaurus • Ultrasauros

## ◀ ULTRASAUROS
(UL-trah-SAW-ros)

30m • 100t • Jurassic

Over 15m high, *Ultrasauros* was the tallest sauropod, and one of the heaviest. Despite its size, it hatched from an egg only about 20cm long. How did it grow so big? Sauropods ate so much they put on up to 3kg of weight every day – growing a tonne heavier each year! Sauropods kept on growing throughout their life, and some lived for over 100 years!

## *Sauropods:* giant plant-eaters

These four-legged plant-eaters were the longest, tallest and heaviest animals ever to walk on Earth. Sauropods appeared in the Jurassic period, replacing their ancestors the prosauropods (p.58), but by the Cretaceous many types had died out.

Sauropods were stupid and slow-moving, but their size protected them from predators. Sauropods needed to digest 5 tonnes of food each day to keep them going. They swallowed stones to grind up the toughest plants. They also produced a ton of dung each day, and enormous amounts of gas from their rear!

A sauropod's skeleton was like a long bridge, with four thick legs holding up its weight. Its long neck was balanced by the weight of its equally long tail.

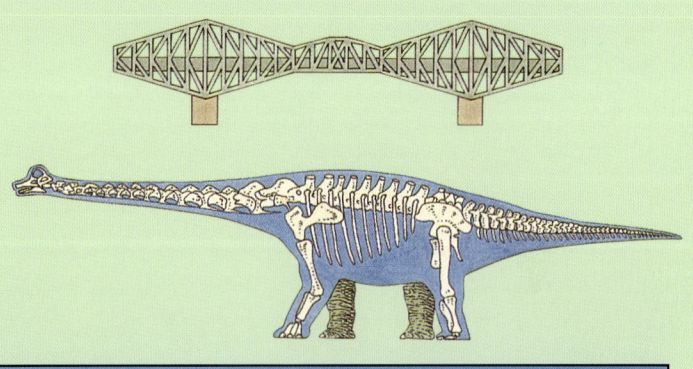

Long necks allowed some sauropods to strip the leaves off the tree tops. Others grazed on low-lying ferns.

Brachiosaurus

Apatosaurus

Diplodocus

87

# U

## UNENLAGIA ▶

(OO-nen-LAY-jia)

4m • 1.5t • Cret.

This fast, ostrich-sized theropod (p.74) is one of the most bird-like dinosaurs ever found. Its shoulders could have moved its short arms in a flapping motion like a flying bird. It could not fly but its arms may have helped it to balance while turning.

## ◀ UTAHRAPTOR

(YOO-tah-RAP-tor) 6.5m • 1t • Cret.

This meat-eating theropod (p.74) was big, fast-moving and agile. It may have hunted in packs, attacking even large sauropods. It had a relatively large brain (p.81) and big eyes, so may have hunted at dusk when the light was low. *Utahraptor* had a 38cm-long claw on the second toe of each foot that it raised off the ground as it ran along.

# V

## VARIRAPTOR ▶

(VA-ri-RAP-tor)

2m • 50kg • Cretaceous

*Variraptor* was a pack-hunter (p.25) about the same size as a human. Discovered in 1998, this theropod (p.74) was one of a family of aggressive hunters called 'dromeosaurs' that included *Microraptor*, *Velociraptor* and *Deinonychus*. *Variraptor* walked on two legs and had a long tail and short arms. It was armed with sharp teeth and vicious claws.

88

# VELOCIRAPTOR ▶

**(vel-OSS-ih-RAP-tor) 2m • 90kg • Cret.**

This highly mobile pack hunter (p.25) had sharp teeth, and savage claws on its hands and feet. It may have been covered with fine feathers to protect it from the heat and cold.

Fossils of *Velociraptor* and *Protoceratops* show how this theropod attacked its prey: the *Velociraptor* grabbed the plant-eater's snout while slashing at its belly with its clawed feet.

## WANNANOSAURUS

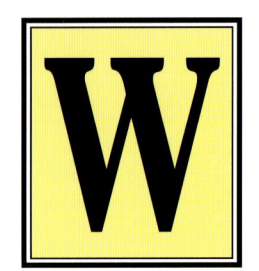

(wan-an-oh-SAW-rus) ▶

1m • 300kg • Cretaceous

*Wannanosaurus* was a tiny plant-eater and one of the bone-headed dinosaurs (p.51). Its thick, flat-topped skull may have been used as a final defence against predators as well as for shoving rival males. It was not a very fast dinosaur, but it ran away from predators if it could.

## ◀ WUERHOSAURUS

(WER-oh-SAW-rus) 7m • 3t • Cretaceous

*Wuerhosaurus* was a plated dinosaur (p.44) whose fossils have been found in China. Like *Stegosaurus*, it had two rows of plates along its back and a pair of spines on its tail.

## ◀ XIAOSAURUS

(SHEE-ah-oh-SAW-rus) 1m • 50kg • Jur.

*Xiaosaurus* was a small, lightly-built ornithopod (p.29). A fast, agile runner, it moved about on two long legs, and had four toes on its feet, five-fingered hands and short arms. Its long, stiff tail helped it to balance as it ran. *Xiaosaurus* had a flexible neck and a small head with large eyes. It sliced up low-growing plants with its leaf-shaped cheek teeth.

# XIPHACTINUS ▶

(zi-FAK-tin-us) 4m • 500kg • Cretaceous

*Xiphactinus* was a bony fish as big as a tuna today. It had short jaws like a bulldog and could swallow a fish as long as a human. Fossils have even been found of a greedy *Xiphactinus* that died when it tried to swallow a prey that was just too big!

## Other creatures

Though archosaurs (p.64) – dinosaurs, pterosaurs and marine reptiles – ruled the Mesozoic era, they lived alongside many smaller creatures. On land were insects, frogs, turtles, snakes, lizards and mammals. In the sea lived fish, squid and ammonites, and by the Cretaceous period, birds and bees had joined the pterosaurs in the air.

**Look out for these creatures:**
- Archaeopteryx, Confuciusornis, Hesperornis, Sinornis – *birds*
- Bavarisaurus – *lizard*
- Cynognathus – *cynodont*
- Echioceras – *ammonite*
- Gerrothorax, Siderops – *amphibians*
- Hybodus – *shark*
- Kannemeyeria – *dicynodont*
- Leedsichthys, Macropoma, Xiphactinus – *bony fish*
- Megazostrodon, Steropodon, Zalambdalestes – *mammals*
- Trilophosaurus – *ancient reptile*

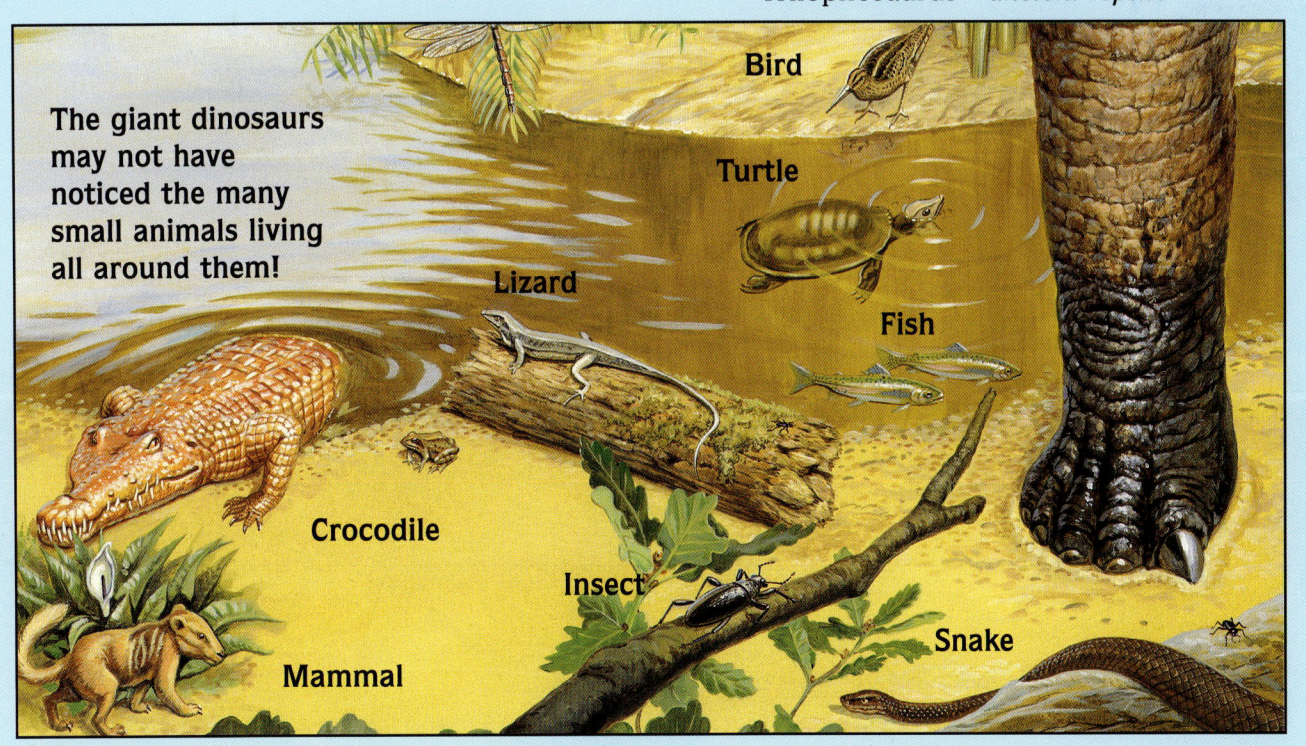

The giant dinosaurs may not have noticed the many small animals living all around them!

# Y

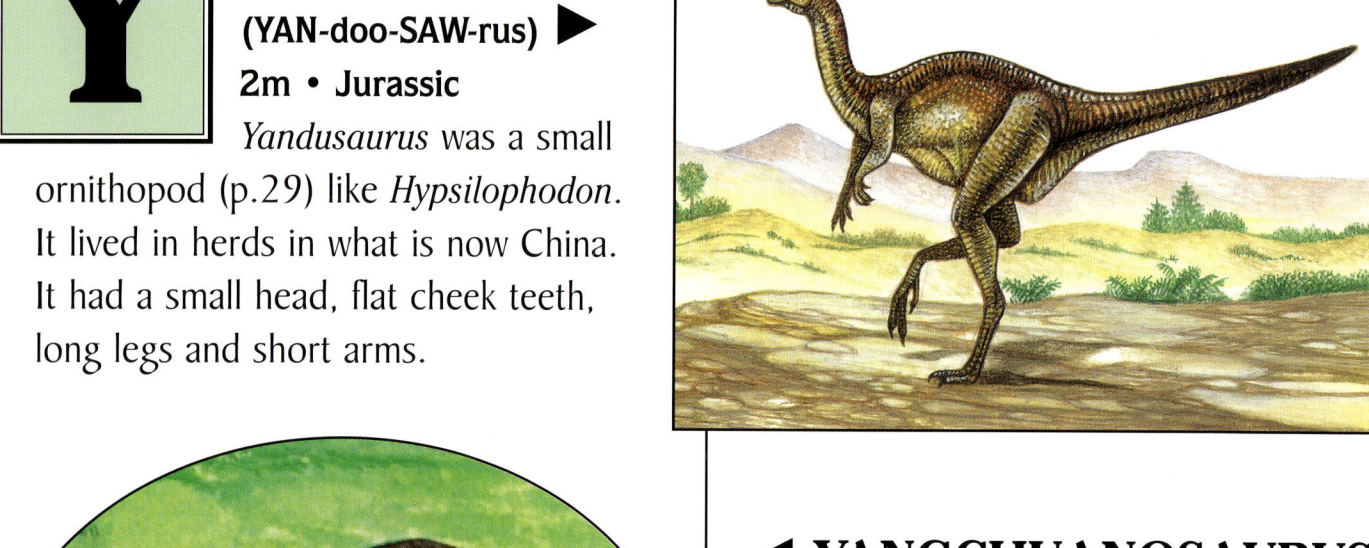

## YANDUSAURUS
(YAN-doo-SAW-rus) ▶
2m • Jurassic

*Yandusaurus* was a small ornithopod (p.29) like *Hypsilophodon*. It lived in herds in what is now China. It had a small head, flat cheek teeth, long legs and short arms.

## ◀ YANGCHUANOSAURUS
(yan-choo-AN-oh-SAW-rus) 10m • 3.5t • Jur.

*Yangchuanosaurus* was a heavy hunter like *Allosaurus* (p.8). It walked on two large, muscular legs. Its huge head housed powerful bone-crunching jaws, which were its chief weapon, though it also had claws on its short arms and on its big, three-toed feet. *Yangchuanosaurus*' heavy tail was about half its total length.

## YAVERLANDIA ▶
(YAV-er-LAND-ee-ah)
1m • 50kg • Cretaceous

*Yaverlandia* is the earliest known bonehead dinosaur (p.51). It is named after the place where it was found: Yaverland Point in southern England. Like other bonehead dinosaurs, or 'pachycephalosaurs', it was a plant-eater that lived in herds.

92

# Z

### ◄ ZALAMBDALESTES
(za-LAM-duh-LESS-teez)

20cm • 100g • Cretaceous

This tiny mammal was a relative of today's shrews. It had large eyes, a long snout and sharp teeth. It hunted for insects at night, when most dinosaurs were resting, but when in danger it could run fast and leap to escape attackers.

### ◄ ZEPHYROSAURUS
(ze-FIRE-oh-SAW-rus)

2m • 100kg • Cret.

*Zephyrosaurus* was a plant-eating ornithopod (p.29) similar to *Hypsilophodon*. It had a small head, flat cheek teeth, long legs and short arms. Its fossils were discovered in North America in 1980.

Zephyrosaurus is named after Zephyr, the Greek god of the west wind.

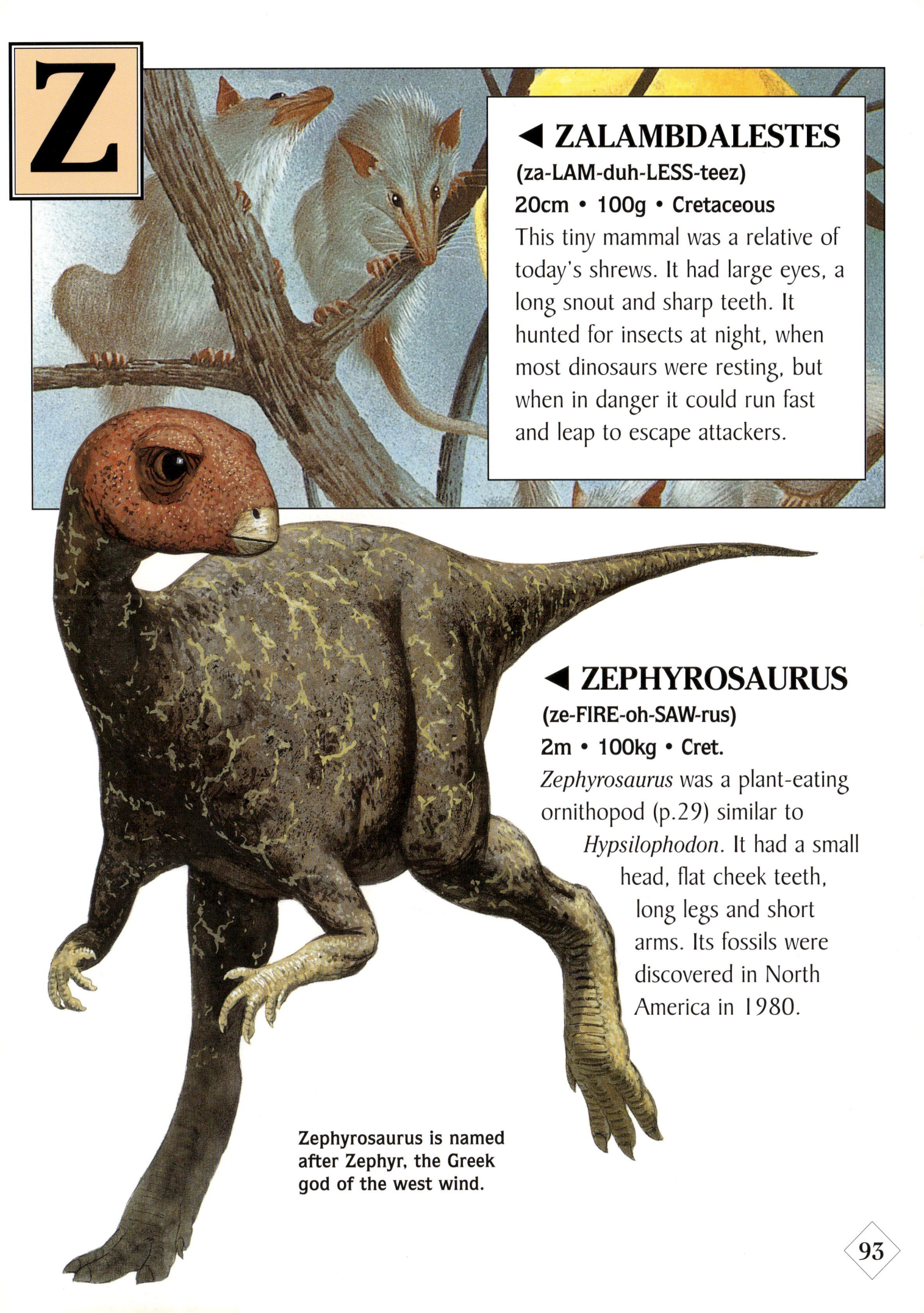

93

# DINOSAUR FAMILY TREE

All dinosaurs belong to one of two groups, depending on the shape of their hips: Saurischia, 'lizard-hipped' dinosaurs, or Ornithischia, 'bird-hipped' dinosaurs (both groups are on p.34). Curiously enough, birds are descended from lizard-hipped dinosaurs!

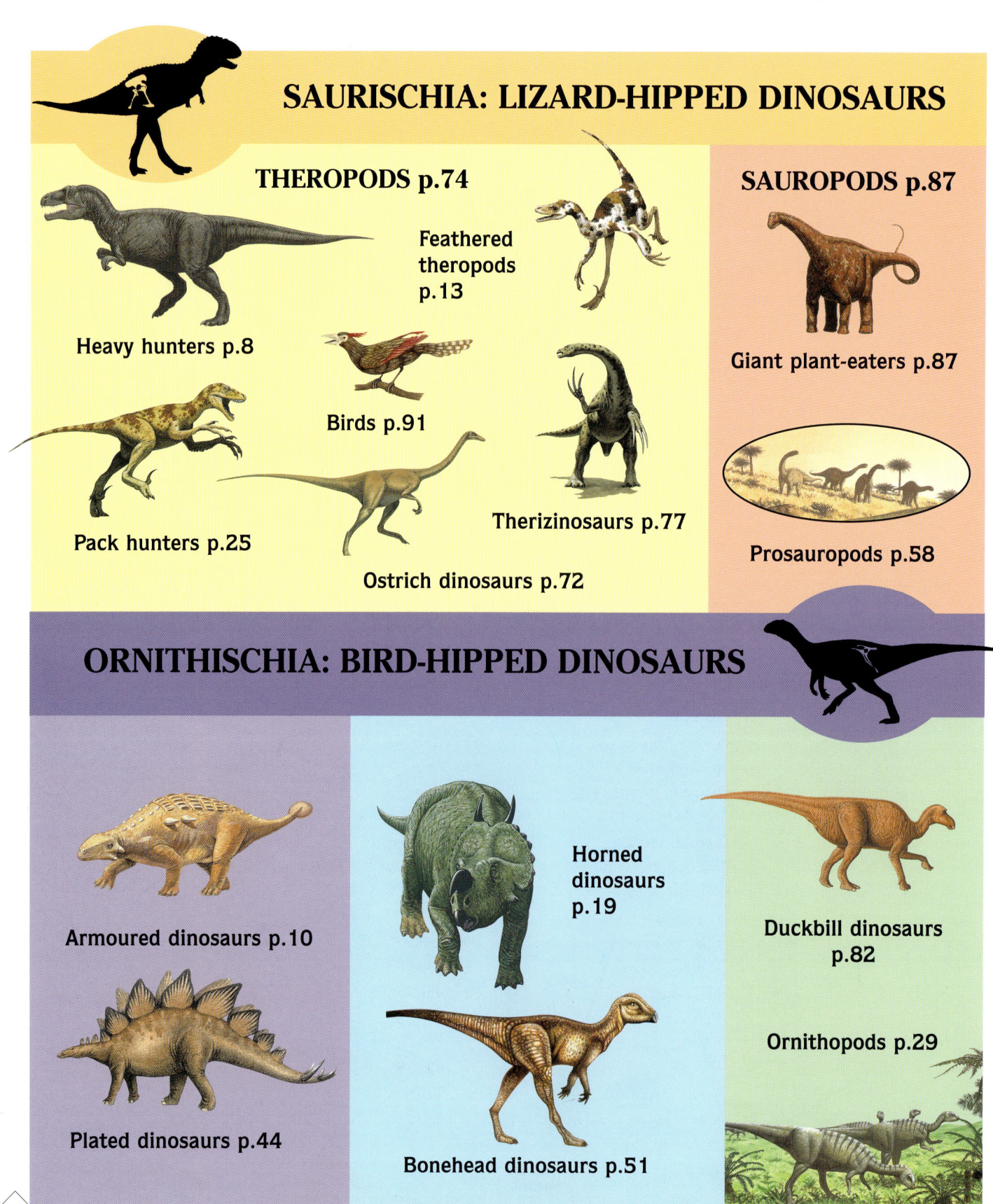

## SAURISCHIA: LIZARD-HIPPED DINOSAURS

### THEROPODS p.74

Heavy hunters p.8

Feathered theropods p.13

Birds p.91

Pack hunters p.25

Ostrich dinosaurs p.72

Therizinosaurs p.77

### SAUROPODS p.87

Giant plant-eaters p.87

Prosauropods p.58

## ORNITHISCHIA: BIRD-HIPPED DINOSAURS

Armoured dinosaurs p.10

Plated dinosaurs p.44

Horned dinosaurs p.19

Bonehead dinosaurs p.51

Duckbill dinosaurs p.82

Ornithopods p.29

94

# INDEX

*Bold numerals show the main entry for each dinosaur. Bold names show special feature boxes.*

Afrovenator **8**
Albertosaurus **8**, 23, 30
Allosaurus **8**, 35, 92
Alxasaurus **9**, 77
Amargasaurus **10**
ammonites 30, 32, 46, 91
amphibians 24, 35, 67, 91
Ankylosaurus **10**
Antarctosaurus **11**
Anurognathus **11**, 15, 60
Apatosaurus 8, **11**, 20, 42, 43, 87
Archaeopteryx **12**, 13, 43, 68
Archelon **12**, 22
**archosaurs 64**
  Ornithosuchus 55
  Saltoposuchus 64
  Sarcosuchus 65
  Sharovipteryx 67
  (see also all dinosaurs, flying reptiles)
**armoured dinosaurs 10**, 94
  Ankylosaurus 10
  Dyoplosaurus 30
  Edmontonia 30
  Euoplocephalus 33
  Hylaeosaurus 38-39
  Minmi 52
  Nodosaurus 54
  Polacanthus 59
  Sauropelta 65
  Scelidosaurus 66
  Talarurus 74
  (see also plated dinosaurs)
Avimimus **12**

Bagaceratops **13**
Bambiraptor **13**
Barosaurus **14**
Baryonyx 7, **14**, 23
Bavarisaurus **14**, 21
birds 4, 5, 7, 12, 13, 21, 36, 43, 68, 91, 94
**bonehead dinosaurs 51**, 94
  Homalocephale 37
  Micropachycephalosaurus 51
  Stegoceras 69
  Wannanosaurus 90

Yaverlandia 92
Brachiosaurus 4, **15**, 87
Brontosaurus *(see Apatosaurus)*

Camarasaurus **16-17**
Carcharodontosaurus **18**
Carnotaurus **18**, 22, 54
Caudipteryx **18**
Centrosaurus **19**
Ceratosaurus **20**, 42, 43
Cetiosaurus **20**
Coelacanth **48**
Coelophysis **20**, 63, 78, 79
Compsognathus 14, **21**
Confuciusornis **21**
Corythosaurus **21**
Cretaceous period 5, **22-23**
crocodiles 4, 7, 64, 65, 91
Cryolophosaurus **24**
cynodonts 24, 91
Cynognathus **24**, 44

Dacentrurus **25**
Daspletosaurus **25**
Deinocheirus **25**
Deinonychus **26-27**, 88
Deltadromeus **28**
dicynodonts 44, 91
Dilophosaurus **43**
Dimorphodon **28**
dinosaur body heat 69
dinosaur brains 81
dinosaur hips 34
dinosaur young 48
Diplodocus 4, 16, **28**, 29, 86, 87
Dryosaurus **29**
Dsungaripterus **30**
**duckbill dinosaurs** 5, **82**, 94
  Corythosaurus 21
  Edmontosaurus 31
  Lambeosaurus 45
  Maiasaura 48
  Parasaurolophus 56-57
  Saurolophus 65
  Tsintaosaurus 82
Dyoplosaurus **30**
**early reptiles** *(see archosaurs)*
Echioceras **30**

Edmontonia **30**, 52
Edmontosaurus 29, **31**
Einiosaurus **31**
Elasmosaurus 12, **32**
Eoraptor **32**, 75, 78
Erlikosaurus **32**
Euoplocephalus 22, 30, **33**, 74

Fabrosaurus **34**
**feathered theropods 13**, 94
  Avimimus 12
  Bambiraptor 13
  Caudipteryx 18
  Incisivosaurus 41
  Microraptor 52
  Sinosauropteryx 68
fish 21, 28, 30, 32, 35, 36, 40, 45, 46, 48, 49, 51, 53, 58, 61, 62, 63, 67, 69, 74, 75, 81, 83, 91
**flying reptiles** 5, **43**, **60**, 64, 91
  Anurognathus 11
  Dimorphodon 28
  Dsungaripterus 30
  Pteranodon 61
  Pterodactylus 61
  Pterodaustro 61
  Quetzalcoatlus 62
  Rhamphorhynchus 63
  Thalassodromeus 75
  Tropeognathus 81
frogs 13, 18, 67, 91

Gallimimus **34**, 75
Gasosaurus **35**
Gerrothorax **35**
**giant plant-eaters** *(see sauropods)*
Giganotosaurus 8, **35**, 75

**heavy hunters 8**, 94
  Allosaurus 8
  Carcharodontosaurus 18
  Carnotaurus 18
  Daspletosaurus 25
  Giganotosaurus 35
  Megalosaurus 50
  Tarbosaurus 74
  Tyrannosaurus rex 84-85

Yangchuanosaurus 92
Herrerasaurus **36**
Hesperornis **36**
Heterodontosaurus **36**, 42, 43, 45
Homalocephale **37**, 51
**horned dinosaurs** 5, **19**, 94
  Bagaceratops 13
  Centrosaurus 19
  Einiosaurus 31
  Protoceratops 59
  Psittacosaurus 59
  Styracosaurus 73
  Triceratops 80
Huayangosaurus **37**
Hybodus **37**
Hylaeosaurus **38-39**, 59
Hypsilophodon **40**, 64, 92, 93

Ichthyosaurus **40**, 46
Iguanodon 4, **41**, 53
Incisivosaurus **41**
insects 11, 12, 15, 18, 22, 28, 50, 67, 68, 72, 91, 93

Janenschia **41**
Jobaria 8, **41**
Jurassic period 5, **42-43**

Kannemeyeria **44**
Kentrosaurus **44**
Kronosaurus 12, **44**, 46

Lambeosaurus 22, 23, **45**
Leaellynasaura **81**
Leedsichthys **45**
Lesothosaurus 29, **45**
Liopleurodon **46-47**
lizards 14, 18, 21, 28, 32, 34, 66, 72, 81, 91

Macropoma **48**
Maiasaura **48**, 82
Mamenchisaurus 4, 42, 43, **49**
mammals 4, 5, 22, 34, 50, 72, 81, 91, 93
marine reptiles 5, 12, 22, 32, 40, 44, 46-47, 51, 53, 54, 64, 83, 91

95

Masiakasaurus 49
Massospondylus **49**, 73
Megalosaurus 42, **50**
Megaraptor **50**
Megazostrodon **50**
Melanorosaurus **51**
Metriorhynchus **51**
Micropachycephalosaurus **51**
Microraptor 7, **52**, 88
Minmi **52**
Mononykus **52**
Mosasaurus 30, 47, **53**
Muraenosaurus 43
Mussaurus **53**
Muttaburrasaurus **53**

Nemegtosaurus **54**
Noasaurus **54**
Nodosaurus **54**
Nothosaurus **54**

ornithischia **34**, 94
Ornithomimus **55**, 72
*ornithopods* **29**, 94
 Dryosaurus 29
 Fabrosaurus 34
 Heterodontosaurus 36
 Hypsilophodon 40
 Iguanodon 41
 Lesothosaurus 45
 Muttaburrasaurus 53
 Tenontosaurus 75
 Thescelosaurus 77
 Xiaosaurus 90
 Yandusaurus 92
 Zephyrosaurus 93
 *(see also duckbill dinosaurs)*
Ornithosuchus 4, **55**
*ostrich dinosaurs* **72**, 94
 Gallimimus 34
 Ornithomimus 55
 Pelecanimimus 58
 Struthiomimus 72
*other creatures* **91**
Oviraptor **55**

*pack hunters* **25**, 94
 Ceratosaurus 20
 Coelophysis 20

Compsognathus 21
Deinocheirus 25
Deinonychus 26-27
Deltadromeus 28
Megaraptor 50
Noasaurus 54
Troodon 81
Utahraptor 88
Variraptor 88
Velociraptor 89
Pangaea 5, 79
Parasaurolophus **56-57**, 82
Pelecanimimus **58**
*plated dinosaurs* 5, **44**, 94
 Dacentrurus 25
 Huayangosaurus 37
 Kentrosaurus 44
 Stegosaurus 70-71
 Tuojiangosaurus 83
 Wuerhosaurus 90
 Plateosaurus 53, **58**
 Polacanthus 39, **59**
*prosauropods* **58**, 94
 Massospondylus 49
 Melanorosaurus 51
 Mussaurus 53
 Plateosaurus 58
 Riojasaurus 63
 Thecodontosaurus 76
Protoceratops 55, **59**, 89
Psittacosaurus **59**
Pteranodon 23, **61**
Pterodactylus 42, 43, **61**, 63
Pterodaustro **61**
*pterosaurs (see flying reptiles)*

Quetzalcoatlus 22, 60, **62**

Rhamphorhynchus 40, **63**
Riojasaurus 58, **63**, 78, 79

Saltasaurus 11, 22, 54, **64**
Saltoposuchus **64**
Sarcosuchus 64, **65**
saurischia **34**, 94
Saurolophus **65**, 74
Sauropelta **65**

*sauropods* 5, **87**, 94
 Amargasaurus 10
 Antarctosaurus 11
 Apatosaurus 11
 Barosaurus 14
 Brachiosaurus 15
 Camarasaurus 16-17
 Cetiosaurus 20
 Diplodocus 28
 Janenschia 41
 Jobaria 41
 Mamenchisaurus 49
 Nemegtosaurus 54
 Saltasaurus 64
 Supersaurus 73
 Ultrasauros 87
Saurornithoides **66**
Scelidosaurus **66**
Segnosaurus **67**
sharks 37, 91
Sharovipteryx **67**, 79
Siderops **67**
Sinornis **68**
Sinosauropteryx **68**, 74
snakes 22, 91
Spinosaurus **69**
squid 45, 46, 91
Stegoceras 25, **69**
Stegosaurus 44, 69, **70-71**, 80, 81, 90
Steropodon **72**
Struthiomimus **72**
Styracosaurus 4, 19, 22, 23, **73**
Suchomimus 7
Supersaurus **73**
Syntarsus **73**, 79

Talarurus 10, **74**
Tanystropheus **74**
Tarbosaurus 23, **74**
Tenontosaurus **75**
Thalassodromeus 60, **75**
Thecodontosaurus **76**
*therizinosaurs* **77**, 94
 Alxasaurus 9
 Erlikosaurus 32
 Segnosaurus 67
 Therizinosaurus 76
Therizinosaurus **76**

*theropods* **74**, 94
 Afrovenator 8
 Albertosaurus 8
 Baryonyx 14
 Cryolophosaurus 24
 Eoraptor 32
 Gasosaurus 35
 Herrerasaurus 36
 Masiakasaurus 49
 Oviraptor 55
 Saurornithoides 66
 Spinosaurus 69
 Syntarsus 73
 Tarbosaurus 74
 Unenlagia 88
 *(see also birds, feathered theropods, heavy hunters, ostrich dinosaurs, pack hunters, therizinosaurs)*
Thescelosaurus **77**
Torosaurus **77**
Triassic period 5, **78-79**
Triceratops **80**
Trilophosaurus **80**
Troodon 23, **81**
Tropeognathus **81**
Tsintaosaurus **82**
Tuojiangosaurus 43, **83**
turtles 12, 53, 91
Tylosaurus 22, 53, **83**
Tyrannosaurus rex 4, 5, 8, 18, 25, 28, 35, 65, 69, 74, **84-85**

Ultrasauros 86, **87**
Unenlagia **88**
Utahraptor **88**

Variraptor **88**
Velociraptor 25, 54, 74, **88**, **89**

Wannanosaurus **90**
Wuerhosaurus **90**

Xiaosaurus **90**
Xiphactinus **91**

Yandusaurus **92**
Yangchuanosaurus 43, 49, **92**
Yaverlandia **92**

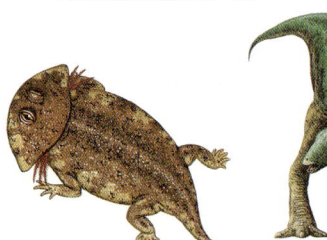

Zalambdalestes **93**
Zephyrosaurus **93**